A Son of the Forest and Other Writings

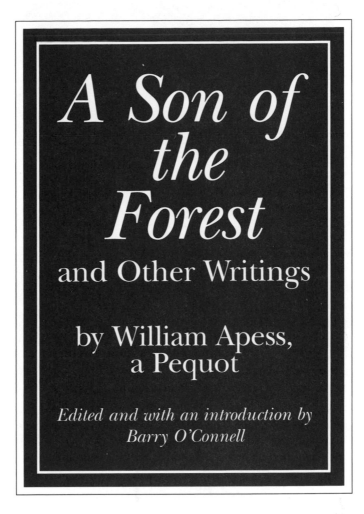

A Son of the Forest

and Other Writings

by William Apess, a Pequot

Edited and with an introduction by
Barry O'Connell

University of Massachusetts Press   *Amherst*

Frontispiece: Portrait of William Apess.

Courtesy, American Antiquarian Society

Copyright © 1992, 1997 by

The University of Massachusetts Press

All rights reserved

Printed in the United States of America

LC 97–20126

ISBN 1–55849–107–4

Designed by Mary Mendell

Printed and bound by Thomson-Shore, Inc.

Library of Congress Cataloging-in-Publication Data

Apess, William, b. 1798.

A son of the forest and other writings / by William Apess, a

Pequot ; edited and with an introduction by Barry O'Connell.

p.   cm.

Includes bibliographical references and index.

ISBN 1–55849–107–4 (pbk. : alk. paper)

1. Apess, William, b. 1798.   2. Pequot Indians — Biography.

3. Indians of North America — New England.   4. Methodist Church —

New England — Clergy — Biography.   5. Indians, Treatment of — New

England.   I. O'Connell, Barry, 1943–   .   II. Title.

E99.P53A3   1997

974'.00497 — dc21   97–20126

CIP

British Library Cataloguing in Publication data are available.

For my mother

Contents

Introduction

As soon as we begin to talk about equal rights, the cry of amalgamation is set up, as if men of color could not enjoy their natural rights without any necessity for intermarriage between the sons and daughters of the two races. Strange, strange indeed! Does it follow that the Indian or the African must go to the judge on his bench, or to the governor, senator, or indeed any other man, to ask for a helpmeet. . . . I promise all concerned that we . . . have less inclination to seek their daughters than they have to seek ours. Should the worst come to the worst, does the proud white think that a dark skin is less honorable in the sight of God than his own beautiful hide? All are alike, the sheep of his pasture and the workmanship of his hands. To say they are not alike to him is an insult to his justice. Who shall dare to call that in question? — William Apess, A Pequot, 1835

It is William Apess's voice that will first strike a reader new to him and that continues to resonate among those who have begun to know his literary work well. Here, in this short passage from *Indian Nullification of the Unconstitutional Laws of Massachusetts*, Apess's commentary on the Mashpee Revolt of 1833–34, one finds many of the characteristics that so distinguish his political and writing presence in Jacksonian America. Its directness and the skillful use of ironically rhetorical questions give some sense of the oratorical power that made him such a famous and controversial public speaker for his brief time in the public eye. His uncompromising indictment of the denial of equality to people of color sounds an especially modern note and comes even before the full emergence of the abolitionist movement (which did not, it should be noted, so dependably link the two peoples).

Here, in this passage, Apess also unhesitatingly taunts white Americans for their hypocrisy and their obsession with miscegenation. It is not, after all, he says, Indians or Africans who lust after white women, but white men who traduce women of color. He pushes yet further, in the deliberate titillation of his play on skin, and also in his rejection of white notions of beauty. His most radical move is to base this egalitarianism firmly on a reading of Christianity at odds with virtually all of its institutionalized forms and practices in antebellum United States.

His militant consciousness is not only surprising in its modern ring; it also challenges the still common assumption that most Indians had disappeared from southern New England by the nineteenth century. From what sources or experiences did Apess derive his consciousness, a consciousness that anticipates so strikingly pan-Indianism and the political sensibility signified in the 1980s and 1990s by the term "people of color"? Unless one resorts to a dubious claim of solitary genius, Apess's militance and his eloquence might best direct historians of this period to look for a developing culture of dissent among New England Indians, African Americans, and very possibly some poor whites located, most probably, in the cities of the region and at least initially supporting itself in the most egalitarian forms of evangelical Christianity then available.

William Apess's achievements as a writer and an activist were little known until recently; indeed it is no exaggeration to say that his writings had no presence in the published history of American literature, just as his importance as a historical actor received no acknowledgment in any standard history. Though his time in the public eye lasted no more than ten years, he managed to write and publish his autobiography and four other substantial works between 1829 and 1836, three of which went into second editions. He seems to have been the first Native American to publish his autobiography; he was assuredly the first to create such a substantial body of publications. At the same time, he traveled as an itinerant preacher and activist throughout New England and New York. As he did, he supported communities of other Indians who, often gathered with African Americans and poor whites to worship, were despised by most whites and represented as nothing more than the dying remnant of a once noble people. And he led the Mashpee Revolt, now largely unknown but significant as one of the first major Indian rights movements. The Mashpee Indians on Cape Cod won the right to govern themselves, in good measure because of Apess's talents as a polemical writer and speaker.

Who he was, how he became who he was, are important questions but equally so how we might understand his long being forgotten, unread for over a century and a half, and his being "recovered" in the 1990s, once again heard and read as though his words and his biography have important significance in the efforts, at the end of the twentieth century, to assess these United States and their prospects.

His beginnings could not have been more modest. His birth was not documented and only because he announces it in his autobiography, *A Son of the Forest*, do we know when and where he was born. His parents were both poor laborers, his father a shoemaker and his mother a servant in gentry households before she had her first child. Like most people of their class — Indian, African American, or white — in this period, his parents moved often, in and around Colchester in the Pequot homelands in southeastern Connecticut, to Hartford and up the Connecticut River Valley, and perhaps occasionally south to New York City, to find work or better or more affordable dwelling places. Apess was born January 31, 1798, "where [my father] pitched his tent in the woods" in Colrain, Massachusetts, the first child of William and Candace Apes.[1]

Shortly after the birth of their first son, the couple moved back to Colchester and lived there in what Apess describes as "comparative comfort" for about three years. Then troubles began. The couple began to quarrel, separated, and then moved away, leaving Apess and his siblings with his maternal grandmother and grandfather. Apess tells us no more about either parent's life, except that he did not see his mother again for twenty years. If the birth records for his siblings are correct, then his parents must have reconciled and separated a number of times because his mother was never with his father in the times between 1808 and 1813 when Apess mentions visiting him.

What happened to Apess at his grandparents decisively changed his life. The children often went hungry, their clothes were insufficient to protect them against the cold weather, and they depended on a good-hearted neighbor who brought them milk when times were hardest. One day, within weeks or a few months from the time his parents left, Apess was badly beaten by his grandmother in a drunken rage while his grandfather urged her on. An uncle who lived in the house saved his life and, by petitioning the selectmen of the town of Colchester through a white neighbor, obtained medical assistance and a permanent removal of the young boy from his grandparents. It took Apess nearly a year to recover from the beating. He was then bound out to Mr. Furman, the good neighbor who had brought milk and petitioned the selectmen.

Such an incident might seem only confirmation of powerful stereotypes

---

1. His parents' names appear as "Apes" in all the documents I have examined. I risk the confusion of spelling their names differently than his to remain consistent with those documents. Apess himself changed the spelling from "Apes" to "Apess" very deliberately in the second editions of *The Experiences of Five Christian Indians* (1837) and the *Eulogy on King Philip* (1837). In two of the debt actions brought against him in 1836 and 1837, his name is entered in the plea as "Apess." Since these seem so clearly to represent his choice of how he wanted to be known, I have adopted his own spelling whenever he is named.

His father was also William as we know from several of the documents published as part of the *Indian Nullification* and so the son was sometimes referred to as William, Jr. Establishing who Apess's mother was is more uncertain. According to her son she was from southeastern Connecticut, a full-blooded Pequot whose family had settled, like many other Pequots, in and around Colchester. But I believe that the "Candace Apes" who was owned as a slave and listed as a "Negro" woman by Captain Joseph Taylor of Colchester until he freed her in 1805 at the age of twenty-eight was probably Apess's mother. For more on this complicated matter see *On Our Own Ground: The Complete Works of William Apess, A Pequot* (xxvii–xxviii, n.17).

January 31 was probably not his exact birth day because in the nineteenth century it was common practice for births, especially in rural areas, to be registered at the end of the month.

about poor people's depravity and especially about drunken Indians demoralized by too close contact with white civilization. Apess wrote at a time when his people's very existence was denied in the official rhetoric of the region and when Indians had few dependable ways to protect themselves against whites cheating them of the small amounts of land still left, depriving them of wages legitimately earned, or denying them lodging. To be an Indian was, in most white peoples' perception, to be inescapably inferior.

Apess's narration of his beating demonstrates his sophisticated awareness of whites' assumptions and expectations of Indians and the care he took to tell his life as itself a political act in a struggle for equal rights for people of color. His depiction of the beating is unsparing:

> At a certain time, when my grandmother had been out among the whites, with her baskets and brooms, and had fomented herself with the fiery waters of the earth, so that she had lost her reason and judgment and, in this fit of intoxication, raged most bitterly and in the meantime fell to beating me most cruelly; calling for whips, at the same time, of unnatural size, to beat me with; and asking me . . . question after question, if I hated her. And I would say yes at every question; and the reason why was because I knew no other form of words. Thus I was beaten, until my poor little body was mangled. . . . (*The Experiences of Five Christian Indians*)

At this moment a reader almost instinctively would exclaim in horror, but Apess anticipates the reaction and turns it backward on those of his readers who are white:

> The white man will say, "What cruel creatures, to use children so!" If I could see that this blame was attached to the poor degraded Indians, I should not have one word to say. But when not a whit of it belongs to them, I have the more to say. My sufferings certainly were through the white man's measure; for they most certainly brought spirituous liquors first among my people. (Ibid.)

Having framed his telling of the story in the context of an account of white people's racism against Indians, Apess also invites readers to struggle with what might have driven his grandmother to her rage and drunkenness. How overwhelmingly demeaning must it have been, peddling brooms and baskets to whites, to move a woman to murderous rage against her grandson?

The Furmans provided a home for the boy for about seven years (1802–1809). During this time he received his only formal schooling, six winter terms. At the Furmans he seems not only to have been happy but to have begun to think of them as his family. They had no children of their own and Apess became close to Mrs. Furman and her mother, who lived in the house. But his status was less secure than he thought. Several times Mr. Furman flogged him. When he was eleven Apess was persuaded by another boy at service in the house to run away. His account emphasizes his innocence and naivete: "At this time it was very fashionable for boys to run away. . . . I thought it was a very pretty notion to be a man — to *do business for myself and become rich.* Like a fool, I concluded to make the experiment and accordingly began to pack up my clothes as deliberately as could be" (*A Son of the Forest*). Mr. Furman caught him before he could make off and questioned him about his intentions. Despite Apess's protestations, Furman decided to sell his indentures to Judge William Hillhouse, a prominent gentleman in the county.[2] Apess agreed to this, thinking that after two weeks he would be free to return. His characterization years later of what happened when he did so speaks his shock and his sense of betrayal by those he had come to accept as family: "The joy I felt on returning home, as I hoped, was turned to sorrow on being informed that I had been *sold* to the judge and must instantly return. This I was compelled to do."

This moment marks in the autobiographical accounts the end of Apess's childhood. His stay at the Hillhouses was brief. He ran away several times and generally rebelled in any way he could against what he took to be their arbitrary authority. After six months, his indentures were again sold — to William Williams in the city of New London, another member of the Connecticut gentry.[3] He was eleven and a half years old.

At first he was well treated, lightly worked, clothed, and fed properly. And he liked living in a bustling city for the first time: "The finery and show caught my eye and captivated my heart" (*A Son*). For about two or three years, his life in the household went well. Religion and class ruptured the tenuous bonds of good feeling that apparently softened the fundamentally economic nature of Apess's indenture. Spiritual strivings which had begun under Mrs. Furman's Baptist tutelage were stirred into deep Christian conviction while he was at the Williamses. Methodists began holding meetings in the neighborhood, and Apess went. Their efforts stirred up a religious revival, and Apess experienced his religious conversion on March 15, 1813, a date he marks as exactly and carefully as he does his birth date. The Williamses were Congregationalists, an inevitability given their elite position, and they objected to Methodist practices

2. Judge William Hillhouse of New London County, chief judge of the county court. He was one of the most prominent and powerful of the old Connecticut gentry. He had fought in the Revolution and had sat in the Continental Congress.

3. The Williamses were the most powerful and extended family in the Connecticut River Valley in these years. This William Williams was also a judge, and a bit after buying Apess's indenture, he became an appointed overseer of the few remaining acres of land belonging to the Mashantucket Pequots.

and the indiscriminate mixing at their meetings of different racial and class groups. Methodism was, at this time in New England, significantly antiestablishment, especially in its successful appeal to the disenfranchised. Apess was forbidden to continue to attend meetings and began to be beaten often for disobeying and other offenses.

His solution was again to run away, in late March or April 1813. Afraid of being caught and brought back, he made his way to New York City, where he found lodgings and a job. Hearing that his master had offered a fifteen-dollar reward for his return, Apess panicked. He met up with a recruiter of militiamen for the War of 1812 and enlisted as a drummer boy. Only fifteen, short and slight of build, he had to lie about his age to enlist. On the march north to Plattsburgh he was forcibly converted into a regular infantryman. Believing this violated the terms of his enlistment and feeling homesick for his father, he tried to desert. Caught but not punished, he was involved in several of the abortive efforts to capture Montreal and fought in the far more glorious (for the Americans) Battle of Lake Champlain on September 11, 1814. Sometime around the middle of March 1815, it seems from his account, he released himself from the army.[4]

Unsheltered as he was in many ways during his years of indenture, combat service was yet an abrupt and tumultuous induction into adulthood. For the first time he found himself exposed to a street language constructed of curses and blasphemy, in a world entirely of men for whom alcohol provided the primary means of solace and recreation. Rum became his most dependable companion throughout his time in the army and for the next few years after he left the ranks.[5] For 1815–16, and possibly until 1817, he lived in Canada, part of it with "my brethren, who ornamented the wood with their camps and chanted the wild beasts of prey with their songs" (*Experiences*). Some of the Canadian Indians with whom he stayed were apparently in Quebec, and others were the Mohawks and the Mississauga Ojibwas around the Bay of Quinte in eastern Ontario. Both communities were especially plagued with alcohol in these years, but Apess implies, without ever recounting, that during this period when he was among these "brethren" he gained some affirmative sense of himself as an Indian.

Much of this time, however, he was "addicted to drinking rum" (*A Son*) and

---

4. He is listed in the military records as having deserted September 14, 1815.

5. Lest this fact even tacitly reinforce the stereotype of "drunken Indians," it is helpful to remember how pervasive alcohol and what we would now call alcoholism were throughout American society in these years. Outside the South, moderation or abstinence became one measure of ascendance into the middle class or into the more stable and respectable ranks of the world of artisans, but otherwise drink flowed — and often was even part of the wage structure for many day laborers. Given his social status, Apess could not possibly avoid this exposure.

moved from job to job, working as a baker in Montreal, a farm laborer, a servant, a cook on a lake sloop, and for a merchant. Finally, apparently far gone into alcoholism, he obtained work on a month-long hunting and fishing expedition in order to dry out. His account suggests what shape he was in: "We had very little rum, and that little we found abundantly sufficient. By degrees I recovered my appetite" (*A Son*).

Determined to return "home" to southeastern Connecticut, Apess began that long journey sometime around April 1816. Means of transport were few in any case and going by water, wagon, or horseback required money he did not have. He had repeatedly to stop along the way from Canada to Connecticut and take whatever jobs he could find. The process occupied the better part of the year until he made it as far as Hartford where, instead of going home, he began to drink again. In the spring of 1817, apparently recovered from his latest bouts of drinking and with enough money to buy himself "good clothes," he at last reached the Colchester area and was reunited with his relatives, though not yet with his immediate family. He had been gone so long without word that they thought him dead. For the next year and a half he stayed in the area, working as a hired hand on one or another farm. His spiritual commitments were renewed after a lapse of almost five years. He resumed regular attendance at Methodist meetings and must have again experienced a significant spiritual quickening so that he could accept baptism by immersion at Bozrah, Connecticut, in December 1818.

This journey, his reunion with family, and his conversion at journey's end reveal something of Apess's artfully deliberate shaping of his autobiographical narrative. Only occasional visits to his father are ever mentioned in his account of his eleven years as an indentured servant. He was four years old at the time of his beating and nineteen when he returned from Canada. Given the trauma he experienced at the hands of his own family, it would not be surprising if he had little or no contact with them. But were this so in fact, why would he have taken such trouble to return to southeastern Connecticut which he, seemingly with no reservation, characterizes as "home"? That he also describes finding his way — not to his father or mother who were again in Colrain — but to other family with whom he is reunited, suggests that he had been in far more regular contact with family and quite possibly other Pequots throughout his childhood than he ever directly relates in his two autobiographies.[6]

6. The question of whether he knew the Mohegan-Pequot language belongs here, as well. Apess never directly says anything about knowing the language, although he does, in the *Eulogy on King Philip*, reproduce the Lord's Prayer in what he identifies as Philip's language (which would not have been Mohegan-Pequot but the related Algonquian language of the Wampanoags). More important is other indirect evidence that he had some fluency. Aunt Sally George, the important Pequot elder with

By creating a sharpened impression of his isolation, Apess dramatizes the centrality of his Christian conversion in the two narratives of his life. Yet he also subordinates that conversion to the even more mysterious process, given his apparent alienation, of his affirmation of his identity as a Pequot and his becoming a militant in the cause of equality for Indians and African Americans. He chooses, I would argue, never to give his readers a direct relation of this, his second conversion. One can identify the substantial effect of this shaping on the interpretative possibilities his texts create: becoming Christian and affirming being Pequot are essential to each other. In making these two processes integral, Apess beautifully inverts and undermines the entire ideological complex through which Europeans and their American descendants employed Christianity as a sign of their superiority to peoples of color and as the legitimation of their taking native peoples' lands, and conversion to it as a measure of Indians' distance from "savagery" and their approach to "civilization."

Apess's baptism symbolized a new stability in his life. In the spring of 1819 he went on foot to Colrain, where his father was living, to learn to make shoes. He appears to have settled down there for a while and it is probably during this time that he saw his mother, now reunited to his father, for the first time in twenty years. A new future also beckoned when he felt God's call to exhort and preach, which he began to do. Returning to Connecticut sometime in 1821 he married Mary Wood, a devout Methodist whom he met at meetings there, "a woman of nearly the same color as myself" (A Son), on December 16, 1821.[7]

The years between 1821 and 1829 when Apess published the first edition of A Son of the Forest are only sketched out in it. The Apess family moved about a good deal and Apess held a number of jobs, bookselling among them, compatible with the itinerant life required of a Methodist exhorter and prayer leader. In April 1829, after the more hierarchically organized Methodist Episcopal church

---

whom he lived and preached for a time, spoke at most only broken English and when she led prayer meetings with him she did so in Mohegan-Pequot. Hers, Anne Wampy's, and Hannah Caleb's accounts in *The Experiences* were unquestionably spoken to Apess in Mohegan-Pequot and it is probable that he was their translator. If my surmises are correct, then his possession of the language would also indicate that he had much greater contact with his Pequot family as he was growing up than he describes in the autobiographies.

7. Mary Apess says of herself in *Experiences*: "I was born in Lyme, Conn., A.D. 1788, on the third day of January. My father was a descendant of one of the Spanish islands, or a native of Spain. My mother was an English woman, a descendant of the Woods family of Lyme. My father died when I was small." After his death the family was so poor that Mary had to be bound out. It seems clear that Mary was illegitimate. Her account of her father's origins and Apess's characterization of her color also suggest that her father may have been part Native American and Spanish, or, more likely by this date when most Native Americans in the Caribbean had long since been wiped out, African American with some mixture of Spanish and possibly Native American heritage.

refused him ordination, quite possibly for racist reasons, Apess was formally ordained a minister in the Protestant Methodist church.

Much of importance in these years is unexplained and thus far unknown. How, for instance, did he conceive his first two books? *A Son of the Forest*, entirely autobiographical though it is, has — as I have already suggested — an artful and subtle shape and manifests not only an impressive command of the language, but also of the intellectual culture of Euro-America. *The Experiences of Five Christian Indians* (1833), though partially autobiographical, brilliantly weaves together accounts by other Native Americans of their Christianity with an explicit attack on the racism of white Christians, an attack that denies whites their right to claim the religion either as historically their own or as the grounds for any assertion of superiority. One needs to wonder when Apess actually acquired the practical skills of a writer and the time to use them. And that leaves the equally critical question of how he came to publish them. He could not have published them without some financial backing; who were his backers and how did he come to know them?

The barriers he had to overcome were substantial. Europeans saw their history of print and writing as legitimating their cultural and political dominance. Indians' acquisition of literacy was represented as their acknowledgment of the inferiority of their own cultures, reason enough for many to refuse the opportunity, though from the earliest encounters a significant number did become literate. Many Indians had a linguistic range beyond the vast majority of their European and Euro-American counterparts, speaking at least one European language, often more, along with several Indian languages. But literacy was a larger step. To command it, Native Americans needed to reach across a great body of cultural difference between their own primarily oral cultures and the Euro-American reliance on the written word. Becoming a writer required yet more, especially access to all the institutions of literacy: schools, libraries and books, newspapers and magazines, editors and publishers.

In the early nineteenth century Euro-America did not yet grant universal access to even the first stages of these linked processes to those it acknowledged as its own. The lower orders might be taught enough to read the Bible. So too, but less frequently, might freed and enslaved black people be taught, especially in the North. But such schooling was severely limited for most to the rudiments of literacy. "Indians" inhabited another and more ambivalent category in Euro-Americans' consciousness. As "savages," that is, as uncivilized, untutored nomads, they had no place in the rising republican empire. For some Euro-Americans this meant urging Native Americans to convert to "American" ways, to become individual property-holding farmers and educated, literate citizens. Once so converted they would no longer be distinguishable culturally as "Indians." Others preferred to believe that Indians could never be anything but "savages." Contact with civilization would only mean the loss of whatever virtues belonged to the savage state and the acquisition of the vices of the civilized. For Apess, or for any other Native American, to become literate in this ideological script entailed being represented as in an intermediate state, a location where one was neither Native nor Euro-American but someone, at best, on the edge of degeneracy or complete assimilation. To write as a Native American could then only be an unspeakable contradiction.

If we set aside these ideological obstacles, there remains the question of how Apess achieved such fluency as a writer. He had only six winters of primary education between the ages of five and eleven. He carefully tells us about his limited proficiency as a reader (and thus, necessarily, about his even more limited proficiency as a writer) after his formal education had ended, ironically enough in one of his most canny and witty passages. The anecdote involves Judge Hillhouse, his second "owner": "this good man did not care much about the Indian boy. He wished to hear me read: I could make out to spell a few words, and the judge said, 'you are a good reader.' —I hope he was a better judge at law" (*Experiences*). *A Son of the Forest,* though it has its awkwardnesses in the first edition, is not the writing of a precariously literate or uneducated man, but of one of fairly wide reading with some experience as a writer. When, in the fifteen years after Judge Hillhouse's patronizing compliment, and how did he learn to write with the wit, eloquence, and facility so manifest in his books?

Several possible answers exist but they are all necessarily speculative because Apess himself is silent on the question and so far no scholar has turned up correspondence or recollections of Apess by his contemporaries which might ground such speculation. His commonly migratory life, not only in the army years and after, but also throughout the 1820s, would have made time, setting, and occasion to read and to write scarce indeed. Perhaps he might have gained in literacy when he was at the Williamses, either with support from them or from his Methodist brethren. It seems certain, however, that in the 1820s he had access to libraries—in those days this generally meant to the learned and rich—and that he had one or more patrons who encouraged and financially supported him, as well as helping to subsidize the publication of his books. Because *A Son of the Forest* was copyrighted in New York City and the Methodist conference that ordained him and later made him a missionary to the Pequots was located there, it seems probable that it was in that city he found such support. From whom is a question that remains to further scholarship.

Someone else might be the author of these writings and Apess so only in name. Ghostwriters and other forms of editorial hands were common in the rapidly developing commercial publishing and writing institutions of the United States in the 1820s and 1830s. The success of *The Memoirs of Catharine Brown* (1824), an account of one of the first Cherokee Christians, which was widely distributed through the evangelical networks, might easily have been seen as justification for someone in the New York or Boston publishing scene to take down and edit Apess's reminiscences. Yet there were Native Americans who had written, and some who had published: Samson Occom, Joseph Johnson, Joseph Brant, and Hendrick Aupaumut from the eighteenth century; Catharine Brown herself (though she did not write her *Memoirs*); Elias Boudinot, the Cherokee editor, probably the best known; and David Cusick, the Tuscaroran historian of the Six Nations, from the early nineteenth century.

Two kinds of textual evidence offer more than fair certainty that Apess himself wrote the books published under his name. None of them is prefaced, or authorized, by anyone else, unlike such nearly mandatory testimonials by whites in books by African Americans and by other Native Americans later. Such flourishes were commonplace in books by Indians edited by, or actually written by, whites. Each book by Apess appears as though no one would, or should, find it remarkable that an "Indian" could write a book, especially one that purported to be his autobiography. Apess's uncompromising militancy in his later books and his unhesitant provision in *A Son of the Forest* of the real names of those who dealt badly with him seem further evidence that he controlled the shaping and the content. The consistency in voice and sensibility in, and across, each of the five books argues for a single author. Had there been an author other than Apess, there would be, I am convinced, some internal evidence for that person's identity. The two likeliest candidates, Lydia Maria Child and William Joseph Snelling, wrote out of a consciousness about Native Americans in their work before Apess's, which, though sympathetic, was unmistakably "other." Neither displayed in these or later writings the slightest capacity to mimic persuasively a voice speaking from within a Native American world.

After his ordination and the publication of *A Son of the Forest* in 1829, virtually nothing is known about the four years before Apess arrived in Mashpee, the old Indian town on Cape Cod, in May 1833. He preached, and like all Methodist ministers, did so on a circuit, which would have meant that he was often apart from his wife. They had children, but only three are known of with any certainty. In *A Son of the Forest* he refers to "my little ones" and, in the 1829 edition, to a son whose name was probably William Elisha who, it turns out, has his own fascinating story.[8] Two daughters married brothers named Chummuck

---

8. Through a set of remarkable coincidences I learned several years ago that a number of Apeses (they kept the first spelling of the name) were living on the South Island of New Zealand. One of them had made inquiry of some American tourists about his "famous" American forebear, the "preacher and writer," William Apess. In time I heard from Erwin Apes in New Zealand, the great-grandson of William Apess. His grandfather, William Apess's son, was named William Elisha, at times using William as his first name and at others, Elisha. William Elisha was an American Indian seaman, known in New Zealand, and one imagines in New England as well, for his prodigious strength. On what was probably

in Mashpee, according to local memory, but for the rest, if there were others, and for their names, no record has yet been found.

In 1831 Apess was sent by the New York Annual Conference of Protestant Ministers to preach to the Pequots. His sermon, *The Increase of the Kingdom of Christ,* was also published that year in New York City, so there is some reason to think he may have been in and around the city a good deal, especially because his revised edition of *A Son of the Forest* was also published there in the same year. *The Experiences of Five Christian Indians of the Pequot Tribe,* which was published in 1833, presents some of the fruits of his mission to his people. These several publications, all in all, suggest that he was devoting a substantial amount of time in the four years to reading and writing.

It was initially in his role as a preacher that Apess came to Mashpee, the major surviving Indian town in Massachusetts, and stirred up enough trouble to earn him regional and, briefly, national notoriety. He became immediately involved in the longstanding discontent and struggle within Mashpee against the white overseers imposed on the community by the Commonwealth of Massachusetts. The three men had the power, which they seemed to have exercised freely, to lease out grazing and haying lands to neighboring whites, to grant woodlot rights, to bind out in employment any man, woman, or child in the community, and to control who entered and who could stay in the town. Equally oppressive in the Mashpees' experience was the imposition of a non-Indian minister who controlled the Old Indian Meeting House, preached only to whites, patronized the Mashpees, and denied use of the Meeting House to a Mashpee Baptist minister and his considerable congregation.

Apess's arrival clearly acted as a new catalyst. The Mashpees adopted him into the community, provided him with a house, and granted him farming, fishing, and wood rights. At his urging and probably with his authorship, the community agreed to two petitions: one to the governor of Massachusetts, the second to the Corporation of Harvard College which controlled the appoint-

---

his first voyage on the ship *Ajax* in 1838, William Elisha mutinied with one other sailor "over the inhumane treatment of the ship's boy. They took charge of the firearms and the ship and ordered it put into Port Otago [on the South Island] where they loaded a whaleboat and deserted" (personal correspondence with Erwin A. Apes and the documents he has collected and sent on to me).

Like his father, William Elisha evidently had little tolerance for injustice. One might fairly assume that the ship's boy was a fellow Indian or perhaps an African American and that William Elisha's partner in arms was another Indian, for many New England Indians pursued lives at sea. Eventually Apes married a Maori woman in 1844 and they had seven children. The American side of the story does not end here. William Elisha did not give up his life at sea and for at least another decade he shipped on American ships with home ports in New England. In 1851, for instance, he shipped out of Portland, Maine (personal correspondence with Reginald H. Pitts who has been checking ship records).

ment of the minister. The first, "the Indian Declaration of Independence," proclaimed that after July 1, 1833, "we, as a tribe, will rule ourselves, and have the right to do so; for all men are born free and equal, says the Constitution of the country." The second petition requested the discharge of the white minister and added that the Mashpees had chosen Apess for their minister and that they intended to take control of *their* meetinghouse. The petitions created a dramatic response and for almost a year what Apess called the "Nullification Crisis" played large in the Boston and other regional newspapers. And, after many incidents, including Apess's arrest and imprisonment, the Mashpees won most of their demands. In March 1834 the state legislature granted the citizens of Mashpee the same rights of township self-governance as other citizens and, as a result, the Mashpees controlled the town until the 1960s. The white minister took longer to get rid of, but by 1840 he, too, was gone.[9]

But so, also, was Apess. His last known public appearance was in Boston in 1836 when he twice gave the address that became the *Eulogy on King Philip* (1836), perhaps his most remarkable literary and political performance. He seems to have left Mashpee in 1838, in part as a result of three debt actions which took all his property. From the beginning of his time in Mashpee, neighboring whites had done their best to separate the Mashpees from their new leader, portraying him as an "outside agitator." But nothing is definitively known about what caused the final separation between him and the people he had led so effectively.

The remainder of his story is regrettably brief. A second edition of *The Experiences of Five Christian Indians* appeared in 1837. Sometime thereafter he moved to New York City, a fact known only because he died there on April 10, 1839. Despite the survival of a formal inquest report, the cause of his death is ambiguous. It was evidently sudden and unexpected. He had been boarding, with his wife, for four months at a lodginghouse at 31 Washington Street in Manhattan, owned by a William Garlick. The neighborhood was a respectable one, though in decline. His wife, another boarder, and Catherine Garlick, the daughter of the owner, all testified at the inquest to Apess's basic good nature and behavior. His wife does identify him as "formerly a preacher of the Methodist society" which might imply, but does not establish, that he had been defrocked. The only hint as to how he might have been supporting himself and his wife is a reference to his giving lectures on the history of the Indians and selling his books at them. On Friday April 7, he complained to his wife that he felt unwell. The next day he got some medicine from a Doctor Viers, took it, and went to bed as his usual time. The following morning, most probably because of

9. The best account of most of these events remains Apess's own *Indian Nullification of the Unconstitutional Laws of Massachusetts* (1835).

an adverse reaction to the medicine, he was too weak to get up and dress. That Sunday night a Doctor Atkinson, a "botanic physician" came to see Apess who told him he had a pain in his side and that he had been purging and vomiting for two days. The doctor gave him medicines to purge himself more thoroughly. He died the next day, April 10. The inquest concluded that he died of apoplexy. Reading the report closely indicates at the very least that he was sickened further and finally killed by the medicines given him by the two doctors, evidence not of any plot or discrimination, but only of the woeful state of American medicine in the mid-nineteenth century. Appendicitis and a burst appendix might to a twentieth-century medical eye seem the most probable cause.

The report contains another fascinating bit of information. His wife who testifies is identified by the name Elizabeth and as having been married to him for ten years. What had happened to Mary Apess, his first wife? Ten years would indicate that he and Elizabeth met and married before or during his first sojourn in Mashpee. Who was she?

The notice of his death in the *Greenfield [Massachusetts] Gazette & Mercury* (May 7, 1839), which reprinted parts of the obituaries from the *New York Sun* and the *New York Observer,* commented that "in New York, it appears that for some time past, his conduct had been quite irregular, and he had lost the confidence of the best portions of the community." Because his wife comments in the inquest report that "he has lately been somewhat intemperate" one might conclude that he had again begun drinking regularly. In fact all that we can thus far know with certainty is that he no longer practiced his ministry and had no evident role in a community of native people or among reformers.

Whatever else, William Apess's is a remarkable story. His books, the primary source for most of what is known of it, are themselves more than documents in the history of New England Native Americans. They belong to and in the history of American literature for their polemical mastery and for Apess's inventive use of the autobiographical form. And they may remind us that though the power of wealth and privilege injures and silences many, it cannot control all. Apess's voice and example might well inspire his readers in a new millennium to question the arrangements of power, and those who legitimate them, which now hold sway in our lives.

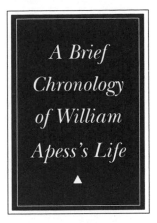

A Brief Chronology of William Apess's Life

▲

1798   Born Colrain, Massachusetts, January 31, the first child of William and Candace Apes.

1801   Parents separate; William placed with his maternal grandparents in Colchester, Connecticut.

1802   Apess's grandmother beats him badly. The town of Colchester binds the boy out to near neighbors, a childless couple, Mr. and Mrs. Furman.

1802–9   From his sixth birthday until his twelfth he attends school during the winter term.

1809   Indenture sold by Mr. Furman to Judge William Hillhouse of New London. Runs away several times. After about six months his indenture again sold—to William Williams in the city of New London.

1809–13   Begins seriously attending Methodist meetings. On March 13, 1813, he has a conversion experience. Runs away to New York City, enlists as drummer boy in a militia unit and goes to the Canadian front, most of the time around Plattsburgh.

1813–15   Involved in several abortive expeditions against Montreal and in the Battle of Lake Champlain, September 11, 1814, when the American forces achieve one of their few victories in the War of 1812. Musters himself out of the army around April or May 1815.

1815–16   Travels to Montreal, upper Canada, Fort Niagara, the Bay of Quinte, and Kingston, holding a variety of temporary jobs, spending some time with his fellow Native Americans in eastern Ontario.

1816–17   In the fall or early winter, starts to return to Connecticut on foot. Reaches the Colchester or Groton, Connecticut, area probably in late April or May 1817.

1818   Baptized by immersion by the Reverend Mr. Barnes.

1819–20   Decides he wishes to see his father again; mother and father have reunited and are living in Colrain. Apess begins to exhort in Methodist class meetings and eventually to preach, though without a license.

1821–24   Returns to Connecticut. Meets and, on December 21, 1821, marries Mary Wood of Salem, Connecticut. The chronology for these years is unclear. The couple live in southeastern Connecticut for a time, and Apess travels to wherever he can find work. At least one child is born in these years, a son, and possibly two daughters.

1825–27   Goes to Providence, Rhode Island, to find work and moves the family there. Becomes a class leader in a local Methodist society. Again begins to exhort and, after some months, is licensed by the Methodists to do so. Decides to become a missionary.

1827–29   Travels around Long Island, the Hudson River valley, Boston, New Bedford, Martha's Vineyard and Nantucket, and north of Boston as an itinerant Methodist exhorter, working much of the time, it seems, with mixed groups of African and Native Americans.

1829   At the April quarterly conference in Utica of the Methodist Episcopal church his request to become a licensed preacher is denied. Joins the more "republican" Protestant Methodists and is ordained by them. Writes *A Son of the Forest* sometime between late 1828 and July 25, 1829, when he deposits copyright title in New York City.

1830   No record of his whereabouts or activities.

1831   Appointed by the New York Annual Conference of the Protestant Methodists to preach to his people, the Pequots. Publishes *The Increase of the Kingdom of Christ*.

1831–33   Little is known about his activities in these years, though he apparently continues to preach to communities of Native Americans and African Americans and also, at least on occasion, to Euro-Americans about the injustices committed against Indians.

1833   Goes to Mashpee for the first time. Mashpee Revolt. Arrested for disturbing the peace, sentenced to jail for thirty days and to pay a hefty fine. *The Experiences of Five Christian Indians; or, An Indian's Looking-Glass for the White Man* published in Boston.

1834   Mashpees granted the right to elect their own selectmen.

1835   *Indian Nullification of the Unconstitutional Laws of Massachusetts* published in Boston.

1836   On January 8 delivers the *Eulogy on King Philip;* repeats it by request on January 26; published in Boston later that same year. In September in a debt action in the Barnstable Court of Common Pleas his name is entered as "Apess."

1837   Second editions of the *Eulogy* and *Experience of Five Christian Indians* published in Boston, by William *Apess.*

1838   Household goods and estate attached by the Barnstable Court of Common Pleas for debt; an inventory of these survives.

1839   Dies in New York City on April 10 of "apoplexy."

A Son of the Forest and Other Writings

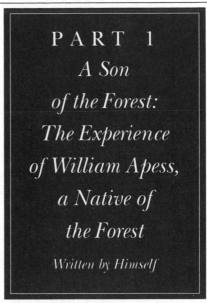

PART 1
*A Son
of the Forest:
The Experience
of William Apess,
a Native of
the Forest*

Written by Himself

A Son of the Forest, published in 1829, was Apess's first book. Internal evidence, however, indicates that it was not his first venture in autobiographical writing. Much of "The Experience of the Missionary" in *The Experiences of Five Christian Indians* (1833) appears to have been composed six months or a year earlier than the longer autobiography. Possibly Apess wrote the first account for a Methodist Conference as part of his request for ordination. A second edition of *A Son of the Forest* was issued in 1831, considerably revised and somewhat rearranged. It is from this edition that the following text has been printed. Because there are, in effect, three different autobiographical accounts from Apess, close comparison of the three can tell us something of importance about his compositional practice and changes in his thinking. Although the 1829 edition of *A Son of the Forest* is not included in this collection, "The Experience of the Missionary" and the 1831 edition of *A Son of the Forest* can be directly and fully compared, and the Textual Note documents the most substantial alterations from the 1829 to the 1831 editions.

When Apess wrote, autobiography was not yet the common literary form it has since become. Accounts of conversion experiences however, were familiar to almost everyone in the early nineteenth-century United States. Oral or written testimony about one's spiritual experience had been mandatory for generations in most Protestant churches. The invention and popularity of revivals from the Great Awakening onward made the practice, along with hymn singing, a generative form in American vernacular cultures. Literary models, especially John Bunyan's *Grace Abounding* (1666) and *Pilgrim's Progress* (1678 and 1684), also played an important role in shaping conventional patterns for such testimony. Bunyan's books were widely distributed in the United States and, along with the Bible, could be found even in those households with few books. Those who could not read would still have known these writings because they were, again like the Bible, often read aloud. A twentieth-century reader approaching these kinds of autobiographies might remember that the language of spiritual concern and regeneration, though it can be formulaic, also can express much of the range of a person's life experience and sensibilities.

   A Son of the Forest deserves attention as one of the earliest—if not *the* earliest—autobiographies written and published by a Native American. This means not only that Apess had few, if any, models for his endeavor but also that one may well see in his book the articulation of issues of identity and the formulation of modes of representation characteristic of later Native American autobiographies.

A
Son
of the
Forest

▲

Preface

In offering to the public a second edition of this work, the Author cannot but testify his gratitude for the liberal patronage bestowed upon the first edition—notwithstanding the many disadvantages under which it appeared. The present edition is greatly improved, as well in the printing as in the arrangement of the work and the style in which it is written. The first edition was hurried through the press, in consequence of which many inaccuracies occurred.

It has been carefully revised; those parts which some persons deemed objectionable have been stricken out;[1] and in its improved form it is now submitted to the public, with the earnest prayer of the author that it may be rendered a lasting blessing to everyone who may give it even a cursory perusal.

1. The objectionable parts appear to be entirely his account of his being rejected as a candidate for ordination in the Methodist Episcopal church and his decision to join the Protestant Methodists, who did ordain him. In the 1829 edition he provides quite lengthy documentation for his conviction that this rejection came because he was an Indian (see Textual Afterword). In this edition, because all of this is excised, the reader does not know that he leaves the Methodist Episcopal church or that he is finally ordained.

Chapter I

William Apess, the author of the following narrative, was born in the town of Colrain, Massachusetts, on the thirty-first of January, in the year of our Lord seventeen hundred and ninety-eight.[1] My grandfather was a white man and married a female attached to the royal family of Philip, king of the Pequot tribe of Indians, so well known in that part of American history which relates

1. January 30 is the date he gives in *The Experiences of Five Christian Indians* (1833).

to the wars between the whites and the natives.[2] My grandmother was, if I am not misinformed, the king's granddaughter and a fair and beautiful woman. This statement is given not with a view of appearing great in the estimation of others—what, I would ask, is *royal* blood?—the blood of a king is no better than that of the subject. We are in fact but one family; we are all the descendants of one great progenitor—Adam. I would not boast of my extraction, as I consider myself nothing more than a worm of the earth.

I have given the above account of my origin with the simple view of narrating the truth as I have received it, and under the settled conviction that I must render an account at the last day, to the sovereign Judge of all men, for every word contained in this little book.

As the story of King Philip is perhaps generally known, and consequently the history of the Pequot tribe, over whom he reigned, it will suffice to say that he was overcome by treachery, and the goodly heritage occupied by this once happy, powerful, yet peaceful people was possessed in the process of time by their avowed enemies, the whites, who had been welcomed to their land in that spirit of kindness so peculiar to the red men of the woods. But the violation of their inherent rights, by those to whom they had extended the hand of friendship, was not the only act of injustice which this oppressed and afflicted nation was called to suffer at the hands of their white neighbors— alas! They were subject to a more intense and heart-corroding affliction, that of having their daughters claimed by the conquerors, and however much subsequent efforts were made to soothe their sorrows, in this particular, they considered the glory of their nation as having departed. (*See Appendix.*)

From what I have already stated, it will appear that my father was of mixed blood, his father being a white man and his mother a native or, in other words, a red woman. On attaining a sufficient age to act for himself, he joined the Pequot tribe, to which he was maternally connected. He was well received, and in a short time afterward married a female of the tribe, in whose veins a single drop of the white man's blood never flowed. Not long after his marriage, he removed to what was then called the back settlements, directing his course first to the west and afterward to the northeast, where he pitched his tent in the woods of a town called Colrain, near the Connecticut River, in the state of Massachusetts. In this, the place of my birth, he continued some time and afterward removed to Colchester, New London County, Connecticut. At

---

2. Apess may be deliberately eliding the two great Indian–English wars in seventeenth-century New England: the Pequot War of 1637 and King Philip's War of 1675–76. But I suspect he has just confused them. Philip was not king of the Pequots, a culture located in the southeastern part of what is now Connecticut, but the sachem of the Pokanokets located in and around Mount Hope in Rhode Island.

the latter place, our little family lived for nearly three years in comparative comfort.

Circumstances, however, changed with us, as with many other people, in consequence of which I was taken together with my two brothers and sisters into my grandfather's family. One of my uncles dwelt in the same hut. Now my grandparents were not the best people in the world—like all others who are wedded to the beastly vice of intemperance, they would drink to excess whenever they could procure rum, and as usual in such cases, when under the influence of liquor, they would not only quarrel and fight with each other but would at times turn upon their unoffending grandchildren and beat them in a most cruel manner. It makes me shudder, even at this time, to think how frequent and how great have been our sufferings in consequence of the introduction of this "cursed stuff" into our family—and I could wish, in the sincerity of my soul, that it were banished from our land.

Our fare was of the poorest kind, and even of this we had not enough. Our clothing also was of the worst description: Literally speaking, we were clothed with rags, so far only as rags would suffice to cover our nakedness. We were always contented and happy to get a cold potato for our dinners—of this at times we were denied, and many a night have we gone supperless to rest, if stretching our limbs on a bundle of straw, without any covering against the weather, may be called rest. Truly, we were in a most deplorable condition— too young to obtain subsistence for ourselves, by the labor of our hands, and our wants almost totally disregarded by those who should have made every exertion to supply them. Some of our white neighbors, however, took pity on us and measurably administered to our wants, by bringing us frozen milk, with which we were glad to satisfy the calls of hunger. We lived in this way for some time, suffering both from cold and hunger. Once in particular, I re-member that when it rained very hard my grandmother put us all down cellar, and when we complained of cold and hunger, she unfeelingly bid us dance and thereby warm ourselves—but we had no food of any kind; and one of my sisters almost died of hunger. Poor dear girl, she was quite overcome. Young as I was, my very heart bled for her. I merely relate this circumstance, without any embellishment or exaggeration, to show the reader how we were treated. The intensity of our sufferings I cannot tell. Happily, we did not continue in this very deplorable condition for a great length of time. Providence smiled on us, but in a particular manner.

Our parents quarreled, parted, and went off to a great distance, leaving their helpless children to the care of their grandparents. We lived at this time in an old house, divided into two apartments—one of which was occupied by my uncle. Shortly after my father left us, my grandmother, who had been out

among the whites, returned in a state of intoxication and, without any provocation whatever on my part, began to belabor me most unmercifully with a
club; she asked me if I hated her, and I very innocently answered in the
affirmative as I did not then know what the word meant and thought all the
while that I was answering aright; and so she continued asking me the same
question, and I as often answered her in the same way, whereupon she
continued beating me, by which means one of my arms was broken in three
different places. I was then only four years of age and consequently could not
take care of or defend myself—and I was equally unable to seek safety in
flight. But my uncle who lived in the other part of the house, being alarmed
for my safety, came down to take me away, when my grandfather made toward
him with a firebrand, but very fortunately he succeeded in rescuing me and
thus saved my life, for had he not come at the time he did, I would most
certainly have been killed. My grandparents who acted in this unfeeling and
cruel manner were by my mother's side—those by my father's side were
Christians, lived and died happy in the love of God; and if I continue faithful
in improving that measure of grace with which God hath blessed me, I expect
to meet them in a world of unmingled and ceaseless joys. But to return:—

The next morning, when it was discovered that I had been most dan-
gerously injured, my uncle determined to make the whites acquainted with
my condition. He accordingly went to a Mr. Furman, the person who had
occasionally furnished us with milk, and the good man came immediately to
see me. He found me dreadfully beaten, and the other children in a state of
absolute suffering; and as he was extremely anxious that something should be
done for our relief, he applied to the selectmen of the town in our behalf, who
after duly considering the application adjudged that we should be severally
taken and bound out. Being entirely disabled in consequence of the wounds I
had received, I was supported at the expense of the town for about twelve
months.

When the selectmen were called in, they ordered me to be carried to Mr.
Furman's—where I received the attention of two surgeons. Some considerable time elapsed before my arm was set, which was consequently very sore,
and during this painful operation I scarcely murmured. Now this dear man
and family were sad on my account. Mrs. Furman was a kind, benevolent, and
tenderhearted lady—from her I received the best possible care: Had it been
otherwise I believe that I could not have lived. It pleased God, however, to
support me. The great patience that I manifested I attribute mainly to my
improved situation. Before, I was almost always naked, or cold, or hungry—
now, I was comfortable, with the exception of my wounds.

In view of this treatment, I presume that the reader will exclaim, "What savages your grandparents were to treat unoffending, helpless children in this cruel manner." But this cruel and unnatural conduct was the effect of some cause. I attribute it in a great measure to the whites, inasmuch as they introduced among my countrymen that bane of comfort and happiness, ardent spirits—seduced them into a love of it and, when under its unhappy influence, wronged them out of their lawful possessions—that land, where reposed the ashes of their sires; and not only so, but they committed violence of the most revolting kind upon the persons of the female portion of the tribe who, previous to the introduction among them of the arts, and vices, and debaucheries of the whites, were as unoffending and happy as they roamed over their goodly possessions as any people on whom the sun of heaven ever shone. The consequence was that they were scattered abroad. Now many of them were seen reeling about intoxicated with liquor, neglecting to provide for themselves and families, who before were assiduously engaged in supplying the necessities of those depending on them for support. I do not make this statement in order to justify those who had treated me so unkindly, but simply to show that, inasmuch as I was thus treated only when they were under the influence of spirituous liquor, that the whites were justly chargeable with at least some portion of my sufferings.

After I had been nursed for about twelve months, I had so far recovered that it was deemed expedient to bind me out, until I should attain the age of twenty-one years.[3] Mr. Furman, the person with whom the selectmen had placed me was a poor man, a cooper by trade, and obtained his living by the labor of his hands. As I was only five years old, he at first thought that his circumstances would not justify him in keeping me, as it would be some considerable time before I could render him much service. But such was the attachment of the family toward me that he came to the conclusion to keep me until I was of age, and he further agreed to give me so much instruction as would enable me to read and write. Accordingly, when I attained my sixth year, I was sent to school, and continued for six successive winters. During this time I learned to read and write, though not so well as I could have wished. This was all the instruction of the kind I ever received. Small and imperfect as was the amount of the knowledge I obtained, yet in view of the advantages I have thus derived, I bless God for it.

3. Being "bound out" was a common practice in New England in the nineteenth century in dealing with people who were indigent, with orphans without relatives willing to take them in, and with those, like Apess, who had been abused. Native Americans, women and children especially, were often bound out—the adults usually for shorter periods, the children often until they reached adulthood. In return for the right to the labor of the indentured, the bondholders undertook to provide food, lodging, and clothing and sometimes other things like education.

CHAPTER II

I believe that it is assumed as a fact among divines that the Spirit of Divine Truth, in the boundless diversity of its operations, visits the mind of every intelligent being born into the world—but the time when is only fully known to the Almighty and the soul which is the object of the Holy Spirit's enlightening influence. It is also conceded on all hands that the Spirit of Truth operates on different minds in a variety of ways—but always with the design of convincing man of sin and of a judgment to come. And, oh, that men would regard their real interests and yield to the illuminating influences of the Spirit of God—then wretchedness and misery would abound no longer, but everything of the kind give place to the pure principles of peace, godliness, brotherly kindness, meekness, charity, and love. These graces are spontaneously produced in the human heart and are exemplified in the Christian deportment of every soul under the mellowing and sanctifying influences of the Spirit of God. They are the peaceable fruits of a meek and quiet spirit.

The perverseness of man in this respect is one of the great and conclusive proofs of his apostasy, and of the rebellious inclination of his unsanctified heart to the will and wisdom of his Creator and his Judge.

I have heard a great deal said respecting infants feeling, as it were, the operations of the Holy Spirit on their minds, impressing them with a sense of their wickedness and the necessity of a preparation for a future state. Children at a very early age manifest in a strong degree two of the evil passions of our nature—*anger* and *pride*. We need not wonder, therefore, that persons in early life feel good impressions; indeed, it is a fact, too well established to admit of doubt or controversy, that many children have manifested a strength of intellect far above their years and have given ample evidence of a good work of grace manifest by the influence of the Spirit of God in their young and tender minds. But this is perhaps attributable to the care and attention bestowed upon them.

If constant and judicious means are used to impress upon their young and susceptible minds sentiments of truth, virtue, morality, and religion, and these efforts are sustained by a corresponding practice on the part of parents or those who strive to make these early impressions, we may rationally trust that as their young minds expand they will be led to act upon the wholesome principles they have received—and that at a very early period these good impressions will be more indelibly engraved on their hearts by the cooperating influences of that Spirit, who in the days of his glorious incarnation said, "Suffer little children to come unto me, and forbid them not, for of such is the kingdom of heaven."

But to my experience—and the reader knows full well that experience is the best schoolmaster, for what we have experienced, that we know, and all the world cannot possibly beat it out of us. I well remember the conversation that took place between Mrs. Furman and myself when I was about six years of age; she was attached to the Baptist church and was esteemed as a very pious woman. Of this I have not the shadow of a doubt, as her whole course of conduct was upright and exemplary. On this occasion, she spoke to me respecting a future state of existence and told me that I might die and enter upon it, to which I replied that I was too young—that old people only died. But she assured me that I was not too young, and in order to convince me of the truth of the observation, she referred me to the graveyard, where many younger and smaller persons than myself were laid to molder in the earth. I had of course nothing to say—but, notwithstanding, I could not fully comprehend the nature of death and the meaning of a future state. Yet I felt an indescribable sensation pass through my frame; I trembled and was sore afraid and for some time endeavored to hide myself from the destroying monster, but I could find no place of refuge. The conversation and pious admonitions of this good lady made a lasting impression upon my mind. At times, however, this impression appeared to be wearing away—then again I would become thoughtful, make serious inquiries, and seem anxious to know something more certain respecting myself and that state of existence beyond the grave, in which I was instructed to believe. About this time I was taken to meeting in order to hear the word of God and receive instruction in divine things. This was the first time I had ever entered a house of worship, and instead of attending to what the minister said, I was employed in gazing about the house or playing with the unruly boys with whom I was seated in the gallery. On my return home, Mr. Furman, who had been apprised of my conduct, told me that I had acted very wrong. He did not, however, stop here. He went on to tell me how I ought to behave in church, and to this very day I bless God for such wholesome and timely instruction. In this particular I was not slow to learn, as I do not remember that I have from that day to this misbehaved in the house of God.

It may not be improper to remark, in this place, that a vast proportion of the misconduct of young people in church is chargeable to their parents and guardians. It is to be feared that there are too many professing Christians who feel satisfied if their children or those under their care enter on a Sabbath day within the walls of the sanctuary, without reference to their conduct while there. I would have such persons seriously ask themselves whether they think they discharge the duties obligatory on them by the relation in which they stand to their Maker, as well as those committed to their care, by so much negligence on their part. The Christian feels it a duty imposed on him to conduct his children to the house of God. But he rests not here. He must have an eye over them and, if they act well, approve and encourage them; if otherwise, point out to them their error and persuade them to observe a discreet and exemplary course of conduct while in church.

After a while I became very fond of attending on the word of God—then again I would meet the enemy of my soul, who would strive to lead me away, and in many instances he was but too successful, and to this day I remember that nothing scarcely grieved me so much, when my mind has been thus petted, than to be called by a nickname. If I was spoken to in the spirit of kindness, I would be instantly disarmed of my stubbornness and ready to perform anything required of me. I know of nothing so trying to a child as to be repeatedly called by an improper name. I thought it disgraceful to be called an Indian; it was considered as a slur upon an oppressed and scattered nation, and I have often been led to inquire where the whites received this word, which they so often threw as an opprobrious epithet at the sons of the forest. I could not find it in the Bible and therefore concluded that it was a word imported for the special purpose of degrading us. At other times I thought it was derived from the term *in-gen-uity*. But the proper term which ought to be applied to our nation, to distinguish it from the rest of the human family, is that of *"Natives"*—and I humbly conceive that the natives of this country are the only people under heaven who have a just title to the name, inasmuch as we are the only people who retain the original complexion of our father Adam.[4] Notwithstanding my thoughts on this matter, so completely was I weaned from the interests and affections of my brethren that a mere threat of being sent away among the Indians into the dreary woods had a much better effect in making me obedient to the commands of my superiors than any corporal punishment that they ever inflicted. I had received a lesson in the unnatural treatment of my own relations, which could not be effaced, and I thought that, if those who should have loved and protected me treated me with such unkindness, surely I had not reason to expect mercy or favor at the hands of those who knew me in no other relation than that of a cast-off member of the tribe. A threat, of the kind alluded to, invariably produced obedience on my part, so far as I understood the nature of the command.

I cannot perhaps give a better idea of the dread which pervaded my mind on seeing any of my brethren of the forest than by relating the following occurrence. One day several of the family went into the woods to gather berries, taking me with them. We had not been out long before we fell in with a company of white females, on the same errand—their complexion was, to say the least, as *dark* as that of the natives. This circumstance filled my mind with terror, and I broke from the party with my utmost speed, and I could not

4. This somewhat inscrutable assertion depends upon Apess's belief that Native Americans were one of the Ten Lost Tribes of Israel. As such, they were "Semites," and thus their complexions were more like Adam's than those of Gentile Euro-Americans.

muster courage enough to look behind until I had reached home. By this time my imagination had pictured out a tale of blood, and as soon as I regained breath sufficient to answer the questions which my master asked, I informed him that we had met a body of the natives in the woods, but what had become of the party I could not tell. Notwithstanding the manifest incredibility of my tale of terror, Mr. Furman was agitated; my very appearance was sufficient to convince him that I had been terrified by something, and summoning the remainder of the family, he sallied out in quest of the absent party, whom he found searching for me among the bushes. The whole mystery was soon unraveled. It may be proper for me here to remark that the great fear I entertained of my brethren was occasioned by the many stories I had heard of their cruelty toward the whites—how they were in the habit of killing and scalping men, women, and children. But the whites did not tell me that they were in a great majority of instances the aggressors—that they had imbrued their hands in the lifeblood of my brethren, driven them from their once peaceful and happy homes—that they introduced among them the fatal and exterminating diseases of civilized life. If the whites had told me how cruel they had been to the "poor Indian," I should have apprehended as much harm from them.

Shortly after this occurrence I relapsed into my former bad habits—was fond of the company of boys—and in a short time lost in a great measure that spirit of obedience which had made me the favorite of my mistress. I was easily led astray, and, once in particular, I was induced by a boy (my senior by five or six years) to assist him in his depredations on a watermelon patch belonging to one of the neighbors. But we were found out, and my companion in wickedness led me deeper in sin by persuading me to deny the crime laid to our charge. I obeyed him to the very letter and, when accused, flatly denied knowing anything of the matter. The boasted courage of the boy, however, began to fail as soon as he saw danger thicken, and he confessed it as strongly as he had denied it. The man from whom we had pillaged the melons threatened to send us to Newgate, but he relented.[5] The story shortly afterward reached the ears of the good Mrs. Furman, who talked seriously to me about it. She told me that I could be sent to prison for it, that I had done wrong, and gave me a great deal of wholesome advice. This had a much better effect than forty floggings—it sunk so deep into my mind that the impression can never be effaced.

I now went on without difficulty for a few months, when I was assailed by fresh and unexpected troubles. One of the girls belonging to the house had taken some offense at me and declared she would be revenged. The better to

5. The nearest Connecticut state prison, named after the famous English prison.

effect this end, she told Mr. Furman that I had not only threatened to kill her but had actually pursued her with a knife, whereupon he came to the place where I was working and began to whip me severely. I could not tell for what. I told him I had done no harm, to which he replied, "I will learn you, you Indian dog, how to chase people with a knife." I told him I had not, but he would not believe me and continued to whip me for a long while. But the poor man soon found out his error, as *after* he had flogged me he undertook to investigate the matter, when to his amazement he discovered it was nothing but fiction, as all the children assured him that I did no such thing. He regretted being so hasty—but I saw wherein the great difficulty consisted; if I had not denied the melon affair he would have believed me, but as I had uttered an untruth about that it was natural for him to think that the person who will tell one lie will not scruple at two. For a long while after this circumstance transpired, I did not associate with my companions.

CHAPTER III

About the time that I had attained my eighth year a sect called the Christians visited our neighborhood.[6] Their hearts were warm in the cause of God— they were earnest and fervent in prayer, and I took great delight in hearing them sing the songs of Zion. Whenever I attended their meetings, which I did as often as possible, I listened to the word of God with the greatest degree of attention. It was not long before I resolved to mend my ways and become a better boy. By my strict attendance on divine worship and my orderly behavior, I attracted the notice of some of the people, who, when they discovered that I was seriously impressed, took me by the hand and strove by every possible means to cheer and encourage me. The notice thus taken of me had a very happy influence on my mind. I now determined to set about the work of repentance. On one occasion the minister addressed the people from a text touching the future state of mankind.

He spoke much on the *eternal happiness* of the righteous and the *everlasting misery* of the ungodly, and his observations sunk with awful weight upon my mind, and I was led to make many serious inquiries about the way of

6. This was probably the group of dissenting Methodists led by James O'Kelly and others who had seceded from the main body in 1793 in a dispute over the power of bishops. They named themselves the Christian Church. They might also have been followers of either Barton Stone or Alexander Campbell, Presbyterians by original training and leaders of the Second Great Awakening marked by the great outdoor camp meetings in the West, at the most famous of which, Cane Ridge, Kentucky, in 1801, Stone preached. Both men separated from the Presbyterians to found the "Christian government," which became formally known as the Christian Church about 1832 (eventually the Disciples of Christ).

salvation. In these days of young desires and youthful aspirations, I found Mrs. Furman ever ready to give me good advice. My mind was intent upon learning the lesson of righteousness, in order that I might walk in the good way and cease to do evil. My mind for one so young was greatly drawn out to seek the Lord. This spirit was manifested in my daily walk; and the friends of Christ noticed my afflictions; they knew that I was sincere because my spirits were depressed. When I was in church I could not at times avoid giving vent to my feelings, and often have I wept sorely before the Lord and his people. They, of course, observed this change in my conduct—they knew I had been a rude child and that efforts were made to bring me up in a proper manner, but the change in my deportment they did not ascribe to the influence of divine grace, inasmuch as they all considered me *too young* to be impressed with a sense of divine things. They were filled with unbelief. I need not describe the peculiar feelings of my soul.

I became very fond of attending meetings, so much so that Mr. Furman forbid me. He supposed that I only went for the purpose of seeing the boys and playing with them. This thing caused me a great deal of grief; I went for many days with my head and heart bowed down. No one had any idea of the mental agony I suffered, and perhaps the mind of no untutored child of my age was ever more seriously exercised. Sometimes I was tried and tempted— then I would be overcome by the fear of death. By day and by night I was in a continual ferment. To add to my fears about this time, death entered the family of Mr. Furman and removed his mother-in-law. I was much affected, as the old lady was the first corpse I had ever seen. She had always been so kind to me that I missed her quite as much as her children, and I had been allowed to call her mother.

Shortly after this occurrence I was taken ill. I then thought that I should surely die. The distress of body and the anxiety of mind wore me down. Now I think that the disease with which I was afflicted was a very curious one. The physician could not account for it, and how should I be able to do it? Neither had those who were about me ever witnessed any disorder of the kind. I felt continually as if I was about being suffocated and was consequently a great deal of trouble to the family, as someone had to be with me. One day Mr. Furman thought he would frighten the disease out of me. Accordingly, he told me that all that ailed me was this: that the devil had taken complete possession of me, and that he was determined to flog him out. This threat had not the desired effect. One night, however, I got up and went out, although I was afraid to be alone, and continued out by the door until after the family had retired to bed. After a while Mr. F. got up and gave me a dreadful whipping. He really thought, I believe, that the devil was in me and supposed that the birch was the best mode of ejecting him. But the flogging was as fruitless as the preceding threat in the accomplishment of his object, and he, poor man, found out his mistake, like many others who act without discretion.

One morning after this I went out in the yard to assist Mrs. Furman milk the cows. We had not been out long before I felt very singular and began to make a strange noise. I believed that I was going to die and ran up to the house; she followed me immediately, expecting me to breathe my last. Every effort to breathe was accompanied by this strange noise, which was so loud as to be heard a considerable distance. However, contrary to all expectation I began to revive, and from that very day my disorder began to abate, and I gradually regained my former health.

Soon after I recovered from my sickness, I went astray, associating again with my old schoolfellows and on some occasions profaning the Sabbath day. I did not do thus without warning, as conscience would speak to me when I did wrong. Nothing very extraordinary occurred until I had attained my eleventh year. At this time it was fashionable for boys to run away, and the wicked one put it into the head of the oldest boy on the farm to persuade me to follow the fashion. He told me that I could take care of myself and get my own living. I thought it was a very pretty notion to be a man—to *do business for myself and become rich*. Like a fool, I concluded to make the experiment and accordingly began to pack up my clothes as deliberately as could be, and in which my adviser assisted. I had been once or twice at New London, where I saw, as I thought, everything wonderful: Thither I determined to bend my course, as I expected that on reaching the town I should be metamorphosed into a person of consequence; I had the world and everything my little heart could desire on a string, when behold, my companion, who had persuaded me to act thus, informed my master that I was going to run off. At first he would not believe the boy, but my clothing already packed up was ample evidence of my intention. On being questioned I acknowledged the fact. I did not wish to leave them—told Mr. Furman so; he believed me but thought best that for a while I should have another master. He accordingly agreed to transfer my indentures to Judge Hillhouse for the sum of twenty dollars.[7] Of course, after the bargain was made, my consent was to be obtained, but I was as unwilling to go now as I had been anxious to run away before. After some persuasion, I agreed to try it for a fortnight, on condition that I should take my dog with me, and my request being granted I was soon under the old man's roof, as he only lived about six miles off. Here everything was done to make me contented, because they thought to promote their own interests by securing my services. They fed

7. Judge William Hillhouse of New London County, chief judge of the county court. He was one of the most prominent and powerful of the old gentry of Connecticut. He had fought in the Revolution and had sat in the Continental Congress. Twenty dollars would have been in 1809, when the transfer occurred, about two months' salary for a common laborer.

me with knickknacks, and soon after I went among them I had a jackknife presented to me, which was the first one I had ever seen. Like other boys, I spent my time either in whittling or playing with my dog and was withal very happy. But I was homesick at heart, and as soon as my fortnight had expired I went home without ceremony. Mr. Furman's family were surprised to see me, but that surprise was mutual satisfaction in which my faithful dog appeared to participate.

The joy I felt on returning home, as I hoped, was turned to sorrow on being informed that I had been *sold* to the judge and must instantly return. This I was compelled to do. And, reader, all this sorrow was in consequence of being led away by a bad boy: If I had not listened to him I should not have lost my home. Such treatment I conceive to be the best means to accomplish the ruin of a child, as the reader will see in the sequel. I was sold to the judge at a time when age had rendered him totally unfit to manage an unruly lad. If he undertook to correct me, which he did at times, I did not regard it as I knew that I could run off from him if he was too severe, and besides I could do what I pleased in defiance of his authority. Now the old gentleman was a member of the Presbyterian church and withal a very strict one. He never neglected family prayer, and he always insisted on my being present. I did not believe or, rather, had no faith in his prayer, because it was the same thing from day to day, and I had heard it repeated so often that I knew it as well as he. Although I was so young, I did not think that Christians ought to learn their prayers, and knowing that he repeated the same thing from day to day is, I have no doubt, the very reason why his petitions did me no good. I could fix no value on his prayers.[8]

After a little while the conduct of my new guardians was changed toward me. Once secured, I was no longer the favorite. The few clothes I had were not taken care of, by which I mean no pains were taken to keep them clean and whole, and the consequence was that in a little time they were all "tattered and torn" and I was not fit to be seen in decent company. I had not the opportunity of attending meeting as before. Yet, as the divine and reclaiming impression had not been entirely defaced, I would frequently retire behind the barn and attempt to pray in my weak manner. I now became quite anxious to attend evening meetings a few miles off: I asked the judge if I should go and take one of the horses, to which he consented. This promise greatly delighted me—but when it was time for me to go, all my hopes were dashed at once, as the judge had changed his mind. I was not to be foiled so easily; I watched the first opportunity and slipped off with one of the horses, reached

8. The issue here is rote prayers, "learned," as opposed to the spontaneous prayer favored by the evangelical Protestants at whose services Apess felt most moved and at home.

the meeting, and returned in safety. Here I was to blame; if he acted wrong, it did not justify me in doing so; but being successful in one grand act of disobedience, I was encouraged to make another similar attempt, whenever my unsanctified dispositions prompted; for the very next time I wished to go to meeting, I thought I would take the horse again, and in the same manner too, without the knowledge of my master. As he was by some means apprised of my intention, he prevented my doing so and had the horses locked up in the stable. He then commanded me to give him the bridle; I was obstinate for a time, then threw it at the old gentleman and run off. I did not return until the next day, when I received a flogging for my bad conduct, which determined me to run away. Now, the judge was partly to blame for all this. He had in the first place treated me with the utmost kindness until he had made sure of me. Then the whole course of his conduct changed, and I believed he fulfilled only one item of the transferred indentures, and that was work. Of this there was no lack. To be sure I had enough to eat, such as it was, but he did not send me to school as he had promised.

A few days found me on my way to New London, where I stayed a while. I then pushed on to Waterford, and as my father lived about twenty miles off, I concluded to go and see him. I got there safely and told him I had come on a visit and that I should stay one week. At the expiration of the week he bid me go home, and I obeyed him. On my return I was treated rather coolly, and this not suiting my disposition, I run off again but returned in a few days. Now, as the judge found he could not control me, he got heartily tired of me and wished to hand me over to someone else, so he obtained a place for me in New London. I knew nothing of it, and I was greatly mortified to think that I was sold in this way. If my consent had been solicited as a matter of form, I should not have felt so bad. But to be sold to and treated unkindly by those who had got our fathers' lands for nothing was too much to bear. When all things were ready, the judge told me that he wanted me to go to New London with a neighbor, to purchase salt. I was delighted and went with the man, expecting to return that night. When I reached the place I found my mistake. The name of the person to whom I was transferred this time was Gen. William Williams, and as my treatment at the judge's was none of the best, I went home with him contentedly.[9] Indeed, I felt glad that I had changed masters and more especially that I was to reside in the city. The finery and show caught my eye and captivated my heart. I can truly say that my situation was better now than it had been previous to my residence in New London. In a little time I was

9. The Williamses were perhaps the most powerful and extensive family in the Connecticut River valley. This William Williams was also a judge, and a bit later than this date, 1809/10, he became an appointed overseer of the Mashantucket Pequots.

furnished with good new clothes. I had enough to eat, both as it respects quality and quantity, and my work was light. The whole family treated me kindly, and the only difficulty of moment was that they all wished to be masters. But I would not obey all of them. There was a French boy in the family, who one day told Mr. Williams a willful lie about me, which he believed and gave me a horsewhipping, without asking me a single question about it. Now, I do not suppose that he whipped so much on account of what the boy told him as he did from the influence of the judge's directions. He used the falsehood as a pretext for flogging me, as from what he said he was determined to make a good boy of me at once—as if stripes were calculated to effect that which love, kindness, and instruction can only successfully accomplish. He told me that if I ever run away from him he would follow me to the uttermost parts of the earth. I knew from this observation that the judge had told him that I was a runaway. However cruel this treatment appeared, for the accusation was false, yet it did me much good, as I was ready to obey the general and his lady at all times. But I could not and would not obey any but my superiors. In short, I got on very smoothly for a season.

The general attended the Presbyterian church and was exact in having all his family with him in the house of God. I of course formed one of the number. Though I did not profess religion, I observed and felt that their ways were not like the ways of the Christians. It appeared inconsistent to me for a minister to read his sermon—to turn over leaf after leaf, and at the conclusion say "Amen," seemed to me like an "empty sound and a tinkling cymbal." I was not benefited by his reading. It did not arouse me to a sense of my danger—and I am of the opinion that it had no better effect on the people of his charge. I liked to attend church, as I had been taught in my younger years to venerate the Sabbath day; and although young I could plainly perceive the difference between the preachers I had formerly heard and the minister at whose church I attended. I thought, as near as I can remember, that the Christian depended on the Holy Spirit's influence entirely, while this minister depended as much upon his learning. I would not be understood as saying anything against knowledge; in its place it is good, and highly necessary to a faithful preacher of righteousness. What I object to is placing too much reliance in it, making a god of it, etc.[10]

---

10. This is an extended comparison of the practices in a revivalist church like the Christians, mentioned earlier, with the more formal rituals of the long-established Presbyterian and Congregational, or "Old Light," congregations. Among the chief differences were the style and manner of preaching—for the revivalist, the written and read text was anathema, representing an overdependence on learning and a lack of faith in the Holy Spirit. The reference to an "empty sound and a tinkling cymbal," echoing the famous passage from 1 Cor. 13:1, is to Isaac Watts's hymn, "Love": "Had I the tongues of Greeks and Jews, / And nobler speech than Angels use, / If

Everything went on smoothly for two or three years. About this time the Methodists began to hold meetings in the neighborhood, and consequently a storm of persecution gathered; the pharisee and the worldling united heartily in abusing them. The gall and wormwood of sectarian malice were emitted, and every evil report prejudicial to this pious people was freely circulated. And it was openly said that the character of a respectable man would receive a stain, and a deep one, too, by attending one of their meetings. Indeed, the stories circulated about them were bad enough to deter people of "character!" from attending the Methodist ministry. But it had no effect on me. I thought I had no character to lose in the estimation of those who were accounted great. For what cared they for me? They had possession of the red man's inheritance and had deprived me of liberty; with this they were satisfied and could do as they pleased; therefore, I thought I could do as I pleased, measurably. I therefore went to hear the *noisy Methodists*. When I reached the house I found a clever company. They did not appear to differ much from "respectable" people. They were neatly and decently clothed, and I could not see that they differed from other people except in their behavior, which was more kind and gentlemanly. Their countenance was heavenly, their songs were like sweetest music—in their manners they were plain. Their language was not fashioned after the wisdom of men. When the minister preached he spoke as one having authority. The exercises were accompanied by the power of God. His people shouted for joy—while sinners wept. This being the first time I had ever attended a meeting of this kind, all things of course appeared new to me. I was very far from forming the opinion that most of the neighborhood entertained about them. From this time I became more serious and soon went to hear the Methodists again, and I was constrained to believe that they were the true people of God. One person asked me how I knew it. I replied that I was convinced in my own mind that they possessed something more than the power of the devil.

I now attended these meetings constantly, and although I was a sinner before God, yet I felt no disposition to laugh or scoff. I make this observation because so many people went to these meetings to make fun. This was a common thing, and I often wondered how persons who professed to be considered great, i.e., "ladies and gentlemen," would so far disgrace themselves as to scoff in the house of God and at his holy services. Such persons let themselves down below the heathen, in point of moral conduct—below the heathen, yes, and below the level of the brute creation, who answer the end for which they were made.

---

love be absent I am found / Like tinkling brass, an empty sound." Watts's great hymns were mainstays of evangelical Protestantism.

But notwithstanding the people were so wicked, the Lord had respect unto the labors of his servants; his ear was open to their daily supplications, and in answer to prayer he was pleased to revive his work. The power of the Holy Ghost moved forth among the people—the spirit's influence was felt at every meeting—the people of God were built up in their faith—their confidence in the Lord of hosts gathered strength, while many sinners were alarmed and began to cry aloud for mercy. In a little time the work rolled onward like an overwhelming flood. Now the Methodists and all who attended their meetings were greatly persecuted. All denominations were up in arms against them, because the Lord was blessing their labors and making them (a poor, despised people) his instruments in the conversion of sinners. But all opposition had no other effect than of cementing the brethren more closely together; the work went on, as the Lord was with them of a truth and signally owned and blessed their labors. At one of these meetings I was induced to laugh; I believe it must have been to smother my conviction, as it did not come from my heart. My heart was troubled on account of sin, and when conviction pressed upon me, I endeavored not only to be cheerful but to laugh, and thus drive away all appearance of being wrought upon. Shortly after this I was affected even unto tears. This the people of the world observed and immediately inquired if I was one of the Lamb's children. Brother Hill was then speaking from this passage of Scripture—*Behold the Lamb of God, that taketh away the sins of the world* [John 1:29]. He spoke feelingly of his sufferings upon the cross—of the precious blood that flowed like a purifying river from his side—of his sustaining the accumulated weight of the sins of the whole world and dying to satisfy the demands of that justice which could only be appeased by an infinite atonement. I felt convinced that Christ died for all mankind—that age, sect, color, country, or situation made no difference. I felt an assurance that I was included in the plan of redemption with all my brethren. No one can conceive with what joy I hailed this *new* doctrine, as it was called. It removed every excuse, and I freely believed that all I had to do was to look in faith upon the Lamb of God that made himself a free-will offering for my unregenerate and wicked soul upon the cross. My spirits were depressed—my crimes were arrayed before me, and no tongue can tell the anguish I felt.

After meeting I returned home with a heavy heart, determined to seek the salvation of my soul. This night I slept but little—at times I would be melted down to tenderness and tears, and then again my heart would seem as hard as adamant. I was greatly tempted. The evil one would try to persuade me that I was not in the pale of mercy. I fancied that evil spirits stood around my bed—my condition was deplorably awful—and I longed for the day to break, as much as the tempest-tossed mariner who expects every moment to be washed from the wreck to which he fondly clings. So it was with me upon the wreck of the world—buffeted by temptations, assailed by the devil, sometimes in despair, then believing against hope. My heart seemed at times almost ready to break, while the tears of contrition coursed rapidly down my cheeks. But sin was the cause of this, and no wonder I groaned and wept. I had often sinned, and my accumulated transgressions had piled themselves as a rocky mountain on my heart, and how could I endure it? The weight thereof seemed to crush me down. In the night season I had frightful visions and would often start from my sleep and gaze round the room, as I was ever in dread of seeing the evil one ready to carry me off. I continued in this frame of mind for more than seven weeks.

My distress finally became so acute that the family took notice of it. Some of them persecuted me because I was serious and fond of attending meeting. Now, persecution raged on every hand, within and without, and I had none to take me by the hand and say, "Go with us and we will do thee good." But, in the midst of difficulties so great to one only fifteen years of age, I ceased not to pray for the salvation of my soul. Very often my exercises were so great that sleep departed from me—I was fearful that I should wake up in hell. And one night when I was in bed, mourning like the dove for her absent mate, I fell into a doze. I thought I saw the world of fire—it resembled a large solid bed of coals—red and glowing with heat. I shall never forget the impression it made upon my mind. No tongue can possibly describe the agony of my soul, for now I was greatly in fear of dropping into that awful place, the smoke of the torment of which ascendeth up forever and ever. I cried earnestly for mercy. Then I was carried to another place, where perfect happiness appeared to pervade every part and the inhabitants thereof. Oh, how I longed to be among that happy company. I sighed to be free from misery and pain. I knew that nothing but the attenuated thread of life kept me from falling into the awful lake I beheld. I cannot think that it is in the power of human language to describe the feelings that rushed upon my mind or thrilled through my veins. Everything appeared to bear the signet of reality; when I awoke, I heartily rejoiced to find it nothing but a dream.

I went on from day to day with my head and heart bowed down, seeking the Savior of sinners, but without success. The heavens appeared to be brass; my prayers wanted the wings of faith to waft them to the skies; the disease of my heart increased; the heavenly physician had not stretched forth his hand and poured upon my soul the panacea of the Gospel; the scales had not fallen from my eyes, and no ray of celestial light had dispelled the darkness that gathered around my soul. The cheering sound of sincere friendship fell not upon my ear. It seemed as if I were friendless, unpitied, and unknown, and at times I wished to become a dweller in the wilderness. No wonder, then, that I was almost desponding. Surrounded by difficulties and apparent dangers, I was resolved to seek the salvation of my soul with all my heart—to trust entirely to the Lord and, if I failed, to perish pleading for mercy at the foot of the throne. I now hung all my hope on the Redeemer and clung with indescribable tenacity to the cross on which he purchased salvation for the *"vilest of the vile."* The result was such as is always to be expected when a lost and ruined sinner throws himself entirely on the Lord—*perfect freedom.* On the fifteenth day of March, in the year of our Lord, eighteen hundred and thirteen, I heard a voice in soft and soothing accents saying unto me, *Arise, thy sins which were many are all forgiven thee, go in peace and sin no more!*

There was nothing very singular (save the fact that the Lord stooped to lift me up) in my conversion. I had been sent into the garden to work, and while there I lifted up my heart to God, when all at once my burden and fears left me—my heart melted into tenderness—my soul was filled with love— love to God, and love to all mankind. Oh, how my poor heart swelled with joy—and I could cry from my very soul, Glory to God in the highest!!! There was not only a change in my heart but in everything around me. The scene was entirely altered. The works of God praised him, and I saw him in everything that he had made. My love now embraced the whole human family. The children of God I loved most affectionately. Oh, how I longed to be with them, and when any of them passed by me, I would gaze at them until they were lost in the distance. I could have pressed them to my bosom, as they were more precious to me than gold, and I was always loath to part with them whenever we met together. The change, too, was visible in my very countenance.

I enjoyed great peace of mind, and that peace was like a river, full, deep, and wide, and flowing continually; my mind was employed in contemplating the wonderful works of God and in praising his holy name, dwelt so continually upon his mercy and goodness that I could praise him aloud even in my sleep. I continued in this happy frame of mind for some months. It was very pleasant to live in the enjoyment of pure and undefiled religion.

Chapter IV

The calm and sunshine did not, however, continue uninterrupted for any length of time; my peace of mind, which flowed as a river, was disturbed. While the adversary tempted me, the fire of persecution was rekindled. It was considered by some members of the family that I was too young to be religiously inclined and consequently that I was under a strong delusion. After a time, Mr. Williams came to the conclusion that it was advisable for me to absent myself entirely from the Methodist meetings.

This restriction was the more galling, as I had joined the class and was extremely fond of this means of grace. I generally attended once in each week, so when the time came round I went off to the meeting, without permission. When I returned, Mrs. Williams prepared to correct me for acting contrary to my orders; in the first place, however, she asked me where I had been; I frankly told her that I had been to meeting to worship God. This reply completely disarmed her and saved me a flogging for the time. But this was not the end of my persecution or my troubles.

The chambermaid was in truth a treacherous woman; her heart appeared to me to be filled with deceit and guile, and she persecuted me with as much bitterness as Paul did the disciples of old. She had a great dislike toward me and would not hesitate to tell a falsehood in order to have me whipped. But my mind was stayed upon God, and I had much comfort in reading the holy Scriptures. One day after she had procured me a flogging, and no very mild one either, she pushed me down a long flight of stairs. In the fall I was greatly injured, especially my head. In a consequence of this I was disabled and laid up for a long time. When I told Mr. Williams that the maid had pushed me down stairs, she denied it, but I succeeded in making them believe it. In all this trouble the Lord was with me, of a truth. I was happy in the enjoyment of his love. The abuse heaped on me was in consequence of my being a Methodist.

Sometimes I would get permission to attend meetings in the evening, and once or twice on the Sabbath. And oh, how thankful I felt for these opportunities for hearing the word of God. But the waves of persecution and affliction and sorrow rolled on, and gathered strength in their progress, and for a season overwhelmed my dispirited soul. I was flogged several times very unjustly for what the maid said respecting me. My treatment in this respect was so bad that I could not brook it, and in an evil hour I listened to the suggestions of the devil, who was not slow in prompting me to pursue a course directly at variance with the Gospel. He put it into my head to abscond from my master, and I made arrangements with a boy of my acquaintance to accompany me.[11] So one day Mr. Williams had gone to Stonington, I left his house, notwithstanding he had previously threatened, if I did so, to follow me to the ends of the earth. While my companion was getting ready I hid my clothes in a barn and went to buy some bread and cheese, and while at the store, although I had about four dollars in my pocket, I so far forgot myself as to buy a pair of shoes on my master's account. Then it was that I began to lose sight of religion and of God. We now set out; it being a rainy night, we bought

11. John Miner, perhaps another indentured servant in the household. He was, in any case, evidently from a poor white family in the vicinity. The two boys would have run away no later than the end of March in 1813.

a bottle of rum, of which poisonous stuff I drank heartily. Now the shadows of spiritual death began to gather around my soul. It was half-past nine o'clock at night when we started, and to keep up our courage we took another drink of the liquor. As soon as we left the city, that is, as we descended the hill, it became very dark, and my companion, who was always fierce enough by daylight, began to hang back. I saw that his courage was failing and endeavored to cheer him up. Sometimes I would take a drink of rum to drown my sorrows—but in vain; it appears to me now as if my sorrows neutralized the effects of the liquor.

This night we traveled about seven miles, and being weary and wet with the rain, we crept into a barn by the wayside, and for fear of being detected in the morning, if we should happen to sleep too long, we burrowed into the hay a considerable depth. We were aroused in the morning by the people feeding their cattle; we laid still, and they did not discover us. After they had left the barn we crawled out, made our breakfast on rum, bread, and cheese, and set off for Colchester, about fourteen miles distant, which we reached that night. Here we ventured to put up at a tavern. The next morning we started for my father's, about four miles off. I told him that we had come to stay only one week, and when that week had expired he wished me to redeem my promise and return home. So I had seemingly to comply, and when we had packed up our clothes, he said he would accompany us part of the way; and when we parted I thought he had some suspicions of my intention to take another direction, as he begged me to go straight home. He then sat down on the wayside and looked after us as long as we were to be seen. At last we descended a hill, and as soon as we lost sight of him, we struck into the woods. I did not see my father again for eight years. At this time, I felt very much disturbed. I was just going to step out on the broad theater of the world, as it were, without father, mother, or friends.

After traveling some distance in the woods, we shaped our course toward Hartford. We were fearful of being taken up, and my companion coined a story, which he thought would answer very well. It was to represent ourselves, whenever questioned, as having belonged to a privateer, which was captured by the British, who kindly sent us on shore near New London; that our parents lived in the city of New York and that we were traveling thither to see them.

Now, John was a great liar. He was brought up by dissipated parents and accustomed in the way of the world to all kinds of company. He had a good memory, and having been where he heard war songs and tales of blood and carnage, he treasured them up. He therefore agreed to be spokesman, and I assure my dear reader that I was perfectly willing, for abandoned as I was I could not lie without feeling my conscience smite me. This part of the business being arranged, it was agreed that I should sell part of my clothing to defray our expenses. Our heads were full of schemes, and we journeyed on until night overtook us. We then went into a farmhouse to test our plan. The people soon began to ask us questions, and John as readily answered them. He gave them a great account of our having been captured by the enemy, and so straight that they believed the whole of it. After supper we went to bed, and in the morning they gave us a good breakfast, and some bread and cheese, and we went on our way, satisfied with our exploits. John now studied to make his story appear as correct as possible. The people pitied us, and sometimes we had a few shillings put into our hands. We did not suffer for the want of food. At Hartford we stayed some time, and we here agreed to work our passage down to New York on board of a brig—but learning that the British fleet was on the coast, the captain declined going. We then set out to reach New York by land. We thought it a good way to walk. We went by way of New Haven, expecting to reach the city from that place by water. Again we were disappointed. We fell in company with some sailors who had been exchanged, and we listened to their story—it was an affecting one, and John concluded to incorporate a part of it with his own. So shortly afterward he told some people that while we were prisoners we had to eat bread mixed with pounded glass. The people were foolish enough to believe us. At Kingsbridge an old lady gave us several articles of clothing. Here we agreed with the captain of a vessel to work our way to New York. When we got under way, John undertook to relate our sufferings to the crew. They appeared to believe it all, until he came to the incredible story of the "glass bread." This convinced the captain that all he said was false. He told us that he knew that we were runaways and pressed us to tell him, but we declined. At length he told us that we were very near to Hellgate (Hurl-gate).—that when we reached it the devil would come on board in a stone canoe, with an iron paddle, and make a terrible noise, and that he intended to give us to him. I thought all he said was so. I therefore confessed that we were runaways—where and with whom we had lived. He said he would take me back to New London, as my master was rich and would pay him a good price. Here the devil prompted me to tell a lie, and I replied that the general had advertised me one-cent reward. He then said that he would do nothing with me further than to keep my clothes until we paid him. When the vessel reached the dock, John slipped off, and I was not slow to follow. In a few days we got money to redeem our clothing; we took board in Cherry Street, at two dollars per week; we soon obtained work and received sixty-two and a half cents per day. While this continued, we had no difficulty in paying our board. My mind now became tolerably calm, but in the midst of this I was greatly alarmed, as I was informed that my master had offered fifteen dollars reward for me and that the captain of one of the packets was looking for me.[12] I dared not go back and therefore determined to go to Philadelphia; to this John objected and advised me to go to sea, but I could find no vessel. He entered on board a privateer, and I was thus left entirely alone in a strange city. Wandering about, I fell in company with a sergeant and a file of men who were enlisting soldiers for the United States Army. They thought I would answer their purpose, but how to get me was the thing. Now they began to talk to me, then treated me to some spirits, and when that began to operate they told me all about the war and what a fine thing it was to be a soldier. I was pleased with the idea of being a soldier, took some more liquor and some money, had a cockade fastened on my hat, and was off in high spirits for my uniform. Now, my enlistment was against the law, but I did not know it; I could not think why I should risk my life and limbs in fighting for the white man, who had cheated my forefathers out of their land.[13] By this time I had acquired many bad practices. I was sent over to Governor's Island, opposite the city, and here I remained some time. Too much liquor was dealt out to the soldiers, who got drunk very often. Indeed, the island was like a hell upon earth, in consequence of the wickedness of the soldiers. I have known sober men to enlist, who afterward became confirmed drunkards, and appear like fools upon the earth. So it was among the soldiers, and what should a child do, who was entangled in their net? Now, although I made no profession of religion, yet I could not bear to hear sacred things spoken of lightly, or the sacred name of God blasphemed; and I often spoke to the soldiers about it, and in general they listened attentively to what I had to say. I did not tell them that I had ever made a profession of religion. In a little time I became almost as bad as any of them, could drink rum, play cards, and act as wickedly as any. I was at times tormented with the thoughts of death, but God had mercy on me and spared my life, and for this I feel thankful to the present day. Some people are of opinion that if a person is once born of the Spirit of God he can never fall away entirely, and because I acted thus, they may pretend to say that I had not been converted to the faith. I believe firmly that, if ever Paul was born again, I was; if not, from whence did I derive all the light and happiness I had heretofore experienced? To be sure it was not to be compared to Paul's— but the change I felt in my very soul.

I felt anxious to obtain forgiveness from every person I had injured in any manner whatever. Sometimes I thought I would write to my old friends and request forgiveness—then I thought I had done right. I could not bear to

12. William Williams began advertising for the return of his runaway indentured servant around the end of April 1813 (*Connecticut Gazette*, April 21, 1813).
13. Against the law because he was actually only fifteen; thus, his enlistment records were falsified to list him as seventeen.

hear any order of Christians ridiculed, especially the Methodists—it grieved me to the heart.

CHAPTER V

It appeared that I had been enlisted for a musician, as I was instructed while on the island in beating a drum. In this I took much delight. While on the island I witnessed the execution of a soldier who was shot according to the decision of a court martial. Two men had been condemned for mutiny or desertion. It is impossible for me to describe the feelings of my heart when I saw the soldiers parade and the condemned, clothed in white, with Bibles in their hands, come forward. The band then struck up the dead march, and the procession moved with a mournful and measured tread to the place of execution, where the poor creatures were compelled to kneel on the coffins, which were alongside two newly dug graves. While in this position the chaplain went forward and conversed with them—after he had retired, a soldier went up and drew the caps over their faces; thus blindfolded, he led one of them some distance from the other. An officer then advanced and raised his handkerchief as a signal to the platoon to prepare to fire—he then made another for them to aim at the wretch who had been left kneeling on his coffin, and at a third signal the platoon fired and the immortal essence of the offender in an instant was in the spirit land. To me this was an awful day—my heart seemed to leap into my throat. Death never appeared so awful. But what must have been the feelings of the unhappy man who had so narrowly escaped the grave? He was completely overcome and wept like a child, and it was found necessary to help him back to his quarters. This spectacle made me serious; but it wore off in a few days.

Shortly after this we were ordered to Staten Island, where we remained about two months. Then we were ordered to join the army destined to conquer Canada. As the soldiers were tired of the island, this news animated them very much. They thought it a great thing to march through the country and assist in taking the enemy's land. As soon as our things were ready we embarked on board a sloop for Albany and then went on to Greenbush, where we were quartered. In the meantime I had been transferred to the ranks. This I did not like; to carry a musket was too fatiguing, and I had a positive objection to being placed on the guard, especially at night.[14] As I had only enlisted for a drummer, I thought that this change by the officer was contrary to law and, as the bond was broken, liberty was granted me; there-

14. Though this may sound like unjustified complaining, it may not when one remembers that Apess was only fifteen, stood five feet, two inches tall, and was slight of build.

fore, being heartily tired of a soldier's life, and having a desire to see my father once more, I went off very deliberately; I had no idea that they had a lawful claim on me and was greatly surprised as well as alarmed when arrested as a deserter from the army. Well, I was taken up and carried back to the camp, where the officers put me under guard. We shortly after marched for Canada, and during this dreary march the officers tormented me by telling me that it was their intention to make a fire in the woods, stick my skin full of pine splinters, and after having an Indian powwow over me, burn me to death. Thus they tormented me day after day.[15]

We halted for some time at Burlington but resumed our march and went into winter quarters at Plattsburgh. All this time God was very good to me, as I had not a sick day. I had by this time become very bad. I had previously learned to drink rum, play cards, and commit other acts of wickedness, but it was here that I first took the name of the Lord in vain, and oh, what a sting it left behind. We continued here until the ensuing fall, when we received orders to join the main army under Gen. Hampton.[16] Another change now took place: We had several pieces of heavy artillery with us, and of course horses were necessary to drag them, and I was taken from the ranks and ordered to take charge of one team. This made my situation rather better. I now had the privilege of riding. The soldiers were badly off, as the officers were very cruel to them, and for every little offense they would have them flogged. One day the officer of our company got angry at me and pricked my ear with the point of his sword.

We soon joined the main army and pitched our tents with them. It was now very cold, and we had nothing but straw to lay on. There was also a scarcity of provisions, and we were not allowed to draw our full rations. Money would not procure food—and when anything was to be obtained the officers always had the preference, and they, poor souls, always wanted the whole for themselves. The people generally have no idea of the extreme sufferings of the soldiers on the frontiers during the last war; they were indescribable; the soldiers ate with the utmost greediness raw corn and everything eatable that fell in their way. In the midst of our afflictions, our valiant general ordered us to march forward to subdue the country in a trice. The pioneers had great difficulty in clearing the way—the enemy retreated, burning everything as they fled. They destroyed everything, so that we could not find forage for the horses. We were now cutting our way through a wilderness

15. All this would have occurred in late summer and fall of 1813.

16. General Wade Hampton was placed at the head of the American troops stationed at Lake Champlain in July 1813. He led one wing of the second of several almost comically inept attempts by the Americans to take Montreal. Hampton resigned from the army in March 1814.

and were very often benumbed with the cold. Our sufferings now for the want of food were extreme—the officers, too, began to feel it, and one of them offered me two dollars for a little flour, but I did not take this money, and he did not get my flour; I would not have given it to *him* for fifty dollars. The soldiers united their flour and baked unleavened bread; of this we made a *delicious* repast.

After we had proceeded about thirty miles, we fell in with a body of Canadians and Indians—the woods fairly resounded with their yells. Our "brave and chivalrous" general ordered a picked troop to disperse them; we fired but one cannon, and a retreat was sounded to the great mortification of the soldiers, who were ready and willing to fight. But as our general did not fancy the smell of gunpowder, he thought it best to close the campaign by retreating with seven thousand men, before a "host" of seven hundred. Thus were many a poor fellow's hopes of conquest and glory blasted by the timidity of one man. This little brush with an enemy that we could have crushed in a single moment cost us several men in killed and wounded. The army now fell back on Plattsburgh, where we remained during the winter; we suffered greatly for the want of barracks, having to encamp in the open fields a good part of the time.[17] My health, through the goodness of God, was preserved notwithstanding many of the poor soldiers sickened and died. So fast did they go off that it appeared to me as if the plague was raging among them.

When the spring opened, we were employed in building forts. We erected three in a very short time. We soon received orders to march and joined the army under General Wilkinson, to reduce Montreal. We marched to Odletown in great splendor, "heads up and eyes right," with a noble commander at our head and the splendid city of Montreal in our view. The city, no doubt, presented a scene of the wildest uproar and confusion; the people were greatly alarmed as we moved on with all the pomp and glory of an army flushed with many victories. But when we reached Odletown, John Bull met us with a picked troop. They soon retreated, and some took refuge in an old fortified mill, which we pelted with a goodly number of cannonballs. It appeared as if we were determined to sweep everything before us. It was really amusing to see our feminine general with his nightcap on his head and a dishcloth tied round his precious body, crying out to his men, "Come on, my brave boys, we will give John Bull a bloody nose." We did not succeed in taking the mill, and the British kept up an incessant cannonade from the fort. Some of the balls cut down the trees, so that we had frequently to spring out of their way when falling. I thought it was a hard time, and I had reason too, as I was in the front of the battle, assisting in working a twelve-pounder, and the British aimed directly at us. Their balls whistled around us and hurried a good many of the soldiers into the eternal world, while others were most horribly mangled. Indeed, they were so hot upon us that we had not time to remove the dead as they fell. The horribly disfigured bodies of the dead—the piercing groans of the wounded and the dying—the cries for help and succor from those who could not help themselves—were most appalling. I can never forget it. We continued fighting till near sundown, when a retreat was sounded along our line, and instead of marching forward to Montreal we wheeled about, and, having once set our faces toward Plattsburgh and turned our backs ingloriously on the enemy, we hurried off with all possible speed. We carried our dead and wounded with us. Oh, it was a dreadful sight to behold so many brave men sacrificed in this manner. In this way our campaign closed. During the whole of this time the Lord was merciful to me, as I was not suffered to be hurt. We once more reached Plattsburgh and pitched our tents in the neighborhood. While here, intelligence of the capture of Washington was received. Now, says the orderly sergeant, the British have burnt up all the papers at Washington, and our enlistment for the war among them; we had better give in our names as having enlisted for five years.[18]

We were again under marching orders, as the enemy, it was thought, contemplated an attack on Plattsburgh. Thither we moved without delay and were posted in one of the forts. By the time we were ready for them, the enemy made his appearance on Lake Champlain, with his vessels of war. It was a fine thing to see their noble vessels moving like things of life upon this mimic sea, with their streamers floating in the wind. This armament was intended to cooperate with the army, which numbered fourteen thousand men, under the command of the captain general of Canada, and at that very time in view of our troops.[19] They presented a very imposing aspect. Their red uniform, and the instruments of death which they bore in their hands, glittered in the sunbeams of heaven, like so many sparkling diamonds. Very fortunately for us and for the country, a brave and noble commander was placed at the head of the army.[20] It was not an easy task to frighten him. For notwithstanding his men were inferior in point of number to those of the enemy, say as one to seven, yet relying on the bravery of his men, he deter-

17. This is General James Wilkinson, who replaced General Henry Dearborn as commander of the American forces on the north shore of Lake Ontario and along the St. Lawrence. This encounter occurred in the fall of 1813 before Wilkinson was relieved of his command in late March. Our "brave and chivalrous general" could have been either Wilkinson or Hampton, though given Wilkinson's reputation it was probably he. Apess's account sounds very much like a description of a skirmish in November 1813, ninety miles from Montreal when a British force of 800 nearly routed Wilkinson's army of some 8,000.
18. Washington was captured and burned on August 24 and 25, 1814.
19. General Sir George Prevost.
20. General Alexander Macomb, who in late August had taken command of the troops at Plattsburgh. His troops were indeed heavily outnumbered by the British.

mined to fight to the last extremity. The enemy, in all the pomp and pride of war, had sat down before the town and its slender fortifications and commenced a cannonade, which we returned without much ceremony. Congreve rockets,[21] bombshells, and cannonballs poured upon us like a hailstorm. There was scarcely any intermission, and for six days and nights we did not leave our guns, and during that time the work of death paused not, as every day some shot took effect. During the engagement, I had charge of a small magazine. All this time our fleet, under the command of the gallant M'Donough, was lying on the peaceful waters of Champlain.[22] But this little fleet was to be taken, or destroyed: It was necessary, in the accomplishment of their plans. Accordingly, the British commander bore down on our vessels in gallant style. As soon as the enemy showed fight, our men flew to their guns. Then the work of death and carnage commenced. The adjacent shores resounded with the alternate shouts of the sons of liberty and the groans of their parting spirits. A cloud of smoke mantled the heavens, shutting out the light of day—while the continual roar of artillery added to the sublime horrors of the scene. At length, the boasted valor of the haughty Britons failed them— they quailed before the incessant and well-directed fire of our brave and hardy tars and, after a hard-fought battle, surrendered to that foe they had been sent to crush. On land the battle raged pretty fiercely. On our side the Green Mountain boys behaved with the greatest bravery. As soon as the British commander had seen the fleet fall into the hands of the Americans, his boasted courage forsook him, and he ordered his army of heroes, fourteen thousand strong, to retreat before a handful of militia.

This was indeed a proud day for our country. We had met a superior force on the lake, and "they were ours." On land we had compelled the enemy to seek safety in flight. Our army did not lose many men, but on the lake many a brave man fell—fell in the defense of his country's rights. The British moved off about sundown.

We remained in Plattsburgh until the peace. As soon as it was known that the war had terminated, and the army disbanded, the soldiers were clamorous for their discharge, but it was concluded to retain our company in the service—I, however, obtained my release. Now, according to the act of enlistment, I was entitled to forty dollars bounty money and one hundred and sixty acres of land. The government also owed me for fifteen months' pay. I have

21. Named after Sir William Congreve (1772–1828), a British artillery specialist. His rocket, invented in 1805, was an important advance in rocket technology. These had a range of up to 9,000 feet and could weigh between eight and forty-two pounds.
22. Captain Thomas Macdonough, thirty years old at the time, a naval officer who led his fleet brilliantly. His victory gave the United States unequivocal control of Lake Champlain and led to the retreat to Canada of the invading British army.

not seen anything of bounty money, land, or arrearages, from that day to this. I am not, however, alone in this—hundreds were served in the same manner. But I could never think that the government acted right toward the "*Natives*," not merely in refusing to pay us but in claiming our services in cases of perilous emergency, and still deny us the right of citizenship; and as long as our nation is debarred the privilege of voting for civil officers, I shall believe that the government has no claim on our services.[23]

CHAPTER VI

No doubt there are many good people in the United States who would not trample upon the rights of the poor, but there are many others who are willing to roll in their coaches upon the tears and blood of the poor and unoffending natives—those who are ready at all times to speculate on the Indians and defraud them out of their rightful possessions. Let the poor Indian attempt to resist the encroachments of his white neighbors, what a hue and cry is instantly raised against him. It has been considered as a trifling thing for the whites to make war on the Indians for the purpose of driving them from their country and taking possession thereof. This was, in their estimation, all right, as it helped to extend the territory and enriched some individuals. But let the thing be changed. Suppose an overwhelming army should march into the United States for the purpose of subduing it and enslaving the citizens; how quick would they fly to arms, gather in multitudes around the tree of liberty, and contend for their rights with the last drop of their blood. And should the enemy succeed, would they not eventually rise and endeavor to regain liberty? And who would blame them for it?

When I left the army, I had not a shilling in my pocket. I depended upon the precarious bounty of the inhabitants, until I reached the place where some of my brethren dwelt.[24] I tarried with them but a short time and then set off for Montreal. I was anxious, in some degree, to become steady and went to learn the business of a baker. My bad habits now overcome my good intentions. I was addicted to drinking rum and would sometimes get quite intoxi-

23. The Treaty of Ghent was signed the day before Christmas, 1814, but news of it did not reach the United States until early February 1815. President Madison sought to maintain a larger peacetime standing army—probably the reason Apess's company was retained in service. He, in fact, mustered himself out no later than September 14, 1815, when his enlistment record notes him as having deserted. Although this may well be the reason he never received pay, bounty, or the land grant, many veterans of the War of 1812 were cheated of these.

24. It seems most likely that these would have been some branch of the Mohawks since Apess was traveling between Plattsburgh and Montreal. However, it is also possible that these were Sokoki, Western Abenakis. Unlike the Mohawk they were Algonquians and, though their language differed from Pequot, Apess and they might still have been able to converse.

cated. As it was my place to carry out the bread, I frequently fell in company, and one day, being in liquor, I met one of the king's soldiers, and after abusing him with my tongue, I gave him a sound flogging. In the course of the affair I broke a pitcher which the soldier had, and as I had to pay for it, I was wicked enough to take my master's money, without his knowledge, for that purpose. My master liked me, but he thought, if I acted so once, I would a second time, and he very properly discharged me. I was now placed in a bad situation—by my misconduct, I had lost a good home! I went and hired myself to a farmer, for four dollars per month. After serving him two months, he paid me, and with the money I bought some decent clothes. By spells, I was hired as a servant, but this kind of life did not suit me, and I wished to return to my brethren. My mind changed, and I went up the St. Lawrence to Kingston, where I obtained a situation on board of a sloop, in the capacity of a cook, at twelve dollars per month. I was on board the vessel some time, and when we settled the captain cheated me out of twelve dollars. My next move was in the country; I agreed to serve a merchant faithfully, and he promised to give me twelve dollars a month. Everything went on smooth for a season; at last I became negligent and careless, in consequence of his giving me a pint of rum every day, which was the allowance he made for each person in his employment.

While at this place, I attended a Methodist meeting—at the time I felt very much affected, as it brought up before my mind the great and indescribable enjoyments I had found in the house of prayer, when I was endeavoring to serve the Lord. It soon wore off, and I relapsed into my former bad habits.[25]

I now went again into the country and stayed with a farmer for one month; he paid me five dollars. Then I shifted my quarters to another place and agreed with a Dutch farmer to stay with him all winter at five dollars a month. With this situation I was much pleased. My work was light—I had very little to do except procuring firewood. I often went with them on hunting excursions; besides, my brethren were all around me, and it therefore seemed like home. I was now in the Bay of Quinte; the scenery was diversified. There were also some natural curiosities. On the very top of a high mountain in the neighborhood there was a large pond of water, to which there was no visible outlet—this pond was unfathomable. It was very surprising to me that so great a body of water should be found so far above the common level of the earth. There was also in the neighborhood a rock that had the appearance of being hollowed out by the hand of a skillful artificer; through this rock wound

25. The chronology is not dependably clear here. Apess probably left the army in Plattsburgh in March or April 1815, by his own account. All these experiences probably occurred between spring 1815 and late summer 1815.

a narrow stream of water: It had a most beautiful and romantic appearance, and I could not but admire the wisdom of God in the order, regularity, and beauty of creation; I then turned my eyes to the forest, and it seemed alive with its sons and daughters. There appeared to be the utmost order and regularity in their encampment.[26]

Oh, what a pity that this state of things should change. How much better would it be if the whites would act like a civilized people and, instead of giving my brethren of the woods "rum!" in exchange for their furs, give them food and clothing for themselves and children. If this course were pursued, I believe that God would bless both the whites and natives threefold. I am bold to aver that the minds of the natives were turned against the Gospel and soured toward the whites because *some* of the missionaries have joined the unholy brethren in speculations to the advantage of themselves, regardless of the rights, feelings, and interests of the untutored sons of the forest. If a good missionary goes among them, and preaches the pure doctrine of the Gospel, he must necessarily tell them that they must "love God and their neighbor as themselves—to love men, deal justly, and walk humbly." They would naturally reply, "Your doctrine is very good, but the whole course of your conduct is decidedly at variance with your profession—we think the whites need fully as much religious instruction as we do." In this way many a good man's path is hedged up, and he is prevented from being useful among the natives, in consequence of the bad conduct of those who are, properly speaking, only "wolves in sheep's clothing." However, the natives are on the whole willing to receive the Gospel, and of late, through the instrumentality of *pious missionaries*, much good has been done—many of them have been reclaimed from the most abandoned and degrading practices and brought to a knowledge of the truth as it is in Jesus!

CHAPTER VII

By many persons great objections have been raised against efforts to civilize the natives—they allege that they have tried the experiment and failed. But how did they make the experiment, and why did they fail? We may with perfect safety say that these persons were prompted to the efforts they made by sinister motives, and they failed because they undertook that in their own strength which nothing short of the power of God could effect. A most

26. Apess's idyll at the Bay of Quinte seems to have occurred in the winter of 1815 and the early spring of 1816. "Brethren," here as elsewhere in his writing, always refers to Native Americans. These "brethren" would have been Mohawks, if Apess was on the northeast side of the bay. There had been a reservation there since 1784. These could have been, were he on the southwest shore, the Mississauga who had a village there.

sweeping charge has been brought against the natives—a charge which has no foundation in truth. It is this, that they are not susceptible of improvement; now, subsequent facts have proved that this assertion is false. Let us look around us, and what do we behold? The forests of Canada and the West are vocal with the praises of God, as they ascend from the happy wigwams of the natives. We see them flocking to the standard of Emmanuel. Many of them have been converted to God and have died in the triumphs of faith. Our religious papers have, from time to time, recorded the blessed effects of the divine spirit—of the strong faith of the expiring Indian. The hopes of the Christian have been elevated, and there is everything to cheer and encourage the followers of the Lamb in so good and noble a cause.

Some people make this charge against the natives, who never knew anything about religion, and I fancy that it would be as difficult for any man who lives in a state of voluptuousness to get to heaven by his own strength as it would be for a native. The Methodists have perhaps done more toward enlightening the poor Indians and bringing them to a knowledge of the truth than all other societies together. I do not say that they did it of their own strength, but that they were the happy instruments in the hands of the Lord Jesus, in accomplishing that which others have failed in performing, as they (the Methodists) relied altogether on the blessing of God. They preached not themselves, but Christ Jesus—and him crucified: And while they were doing this, they sought not their own advancement. And no wonder that they succeeded—the natives were melted down into tenderness and love, and they became as kind and obliging as any people could be.

It is my opinion that our nation retains the original complexion of our common father, Adam. This is strongly impressed on my mind. I think it is very reasonable, and in this opinion I am not singular, as some of the best writers of the age, among whom we find a Clinton, a Boudinot, a West, and a Hinds, have expressed their sentiments in its favor.[27] But to return:

27. The context is Apess's belief that the Indians were descendants of the Ten Lost Tribes of Israel and thus due every respect as creatures as equally in God's favor as Euro-American Christians. This belief attempted to counter the conviction, used by many Euro-Americans to justify their depredations on the Indians, that these were an inferior people incapable of civilization and Christianity. The references are to De Witt Clinton (1769–1828), senator from New York, mayor of New York City, and the governor of the state (1817–23), responsible for the building of the Erie Canal. One of the most important and innovative politicians in the early republic, he was much interested in Native Americans and their origins and wrote about them; see esp. *The Life and Writings* (New York: Baker and Scribner, 1849). Elias Boudinot (1740–1821) was a member of the Continental Congress from New Jersey and the first president of the American Bible Society. The Cherokee editor, Elias Boudinot, was his protégé. The Euro-American Boudinot wrote one of the major texts on this issue, from which Apess took most of the Appendix to *A Son of the Forest*. See Boudinot, *A Star in the West; or, A Humble Attempt to Discover the Long Lost Ten Tribes of Israel* (Trenton,

In the spring the old gentleman set us to making maple sugar. This took us into the woods, which were vocal with the songs of the birds; all nature seemed to smile and rejoice in the freshness and beauty of spring. My brethren appeared very cheerful on account of its return and enjoyed themselves in hunting, fishing, basket making, etc. After we had done making sugar, I told the old gentleman I wished to go and see my friends in the East, as I had been absent about three years: He consented, though he wished me to tarry longer with him. I then went to Kingston, where I fell into bad company, with drunkards. They were friends as long as my money held out, but when that failed, their friendship turned to enmity. Thus all my money was gone, and I was alone and destitute in a strange place. I went to live with a man for a while but had not been with him but a few days before I found much trouble in the wigwam. The lady of the house was a lady indeed; when she went to bed she could not get up without assistance, and very often her husband would mourn over her and say what a wretch he had been ever since he had married her. She was very intemperate, and here I saw the evil of ardent spirits. They soon after broke up housekeeping, and I of course lost my place. I had not refrained from my evil practices, and some of my wicked companions advised me to steal for a living, but as I had no inclination to rob anyone, I had prudence and firmness to resist the temptation. Those who advised me to do so were not my brethren but whites. My eyes were now opened to see my pretended friends in their true light. I concluded that such friends were not useful to me, and I was awakened to reflection and determined to leave their society.

One Sabbath, as I was passing by a chapel, I heard a good man of God giving good advice to his people. He earnestly exhorted them to faithfulness and prayer. I went in, and while listening to his fervent discourse, all my promises of reformation rose up before me. I was very much affected—my spirit was troubled, and I began to think seriously about my situation. The next day I sat down in the sun to sun myself and to consider as to my future course. As I found I was friendless, without money, and without work, the desire of my heart was to get home. While reflecting on this, to me, important subject, it appeared as if God was working for me, as four boatmen about going on a hunting and fishing excursion came to purchase stores. I asked them if I should go with them—they wished to know where I was going, and I

NJ: Fenton, Hutchinson, and Dunham, 1816). West and Hinds I have not been able to identify definitively. West is probably John West (177[?]–1845), who published in 1827 *Journal during a Residence at the Red River Colony British N.A. and Excursions Among the Northwest American Indians* (London: Seeley, 1827). Hinds may be Samuel Hinds, bishop of Norwich (England), whose *History of the Rise and Early Progress of Christianity* (London: Baldwin and Gadock, 1828) might have been available to Apess and which had material relevant to his point here.

told them I was willing to go anywhere. One of them hired me to fish, and I went with them; the time passed rapidly on, and I felt as happy as a king. We had very little rum, and that little we found abundantly sufficient. By degrees I recovered my appetite. I was with these good men upward of a month, part of which time we spent in fishing and part in hunting deer. They then returned to see their families, taking me with them. The one who had hired me to fish, when I told him that I wished to go home, acted like a gentleman and paid me my wages. After purchasing a pair of shoes, I had only one shilling left. I now started for home, a distance of more than three hundred miles.[28] This was a long journey to perform alone, and on foot. But, thank God, I found friends—many who were willing to supply me with food and render me assistance. I had no difficulty until I reached Utica, where I lost my shilling. I was now penniless. Fortunately, I agreed with the captain of a boat to work my passage down the Mohawk River. In this way I got along some distance. When I left the boat I had to beg or work, as answered my purpose best, as I was extremely anxious to get home; therefore, I preferred the shortest method. But nevertheless I refused not to work. But unfortunately the people in this part of the country, seeing I was an Indian, took but little notice of me. I was also exposed to some temptations, as I met often in the road the veriest wretches that defile the earth—such as would forget the dignity of human nature so far as to blackguard me because I was an Indian.[29] A son of the forest would never stoop so low as to offer such an insult to a stranger who happened to be among them. I was much mortified, and believing that they ought to be corrected for so flagrant a breach of good manners and "civilization," I thought seriously, in one or two instances, of inflicting summary punishment; but this feeling gave way to that of pity. It appeared to me as if they had not the sense and wisdom of the brute creation.

When I reached Albany, the bells were tolling. The solemn sound entered into the deepest recesses of my soul, pressed down as it were with a multitude of sorrows. It appeared to be a very solemn time. They were engaged in depositing the mortal remains of a man in the narrow and darksome grave, who had been killed the day before by a stroke of lightning. Oh, how thankful I felt that I had not been taken off instead of that man. I immediately went to Hoosick, passing through the pleasant town of Troy. I was now about one hundred miles from home, and not having clothes suitable for the season, I concluded to go to work in order to get such as would answer

---

28. Kingston, Ontario, to New London or Colchester, Connecticut, would in fact be considerably farther, more on the magnitude of five to six hundred miles.
29. "blackguard": i.e., to revile him.

to make my appearance in at home. So I began to make inquiries for work and come across one Esquire Haviland, who engaged me to help him the remainder of the season, at eight dollars per month. He treated me with the utmost kindness; he took me to church to hear the word of God, dressed me up in good clothes, and took the best care of me while I remained with them. When I left them, instead of going home, as I intended, I steered my course for Old Hartford, where I fell in with some of the rough people of the world, and made a halt. I again listened to the advice of the wicked and turned aside from the path of virtue. I soon agreed to go to sea with one of my new comrades, but we could not ship ourselves. I now got to drinking too much of the accursed liquor again. As we failed in our project at Hartford, we started for New Haven, where I abandoned the notion of going to sea and went to work, and all I got for two months labor was a pair of pantaloons. I thought surely that these were hard times. Winter was now coming on apace, and as I had very little clothing, I had to do the best I could. I saw the impropriety of keeping bad company, and I must in this respect acknowledge that I was a very fool, and only a half-witted Indian—the Lord had often warned me of my danger, and I was advised of the evil consequences by those who I believe were concerned for my welfare here and hereafter.

In the spring I had good clothes, and withal looked very decent, so I thought that I would make another effort to reach my home. In my journey, being in the land of steady habits, I found the people very benevolent and kind. I experienced but very little difficulty on the way, and at last I arrived in safety at the home of my childhood. At first my people looked upon me as one risen from the dead. Not having heard from me since I left home, being more than four years, they thought I must certainly have died, and the days of mourning had almost passed. They were rejoiced to see me once more in the land of the living, and I was equally rejoiced to find all my folks alive. The whites with whom I had been acquainted were also very glad to see me. After I had spent some time with my relations in Groton and visited all my old friends, I concluded to go to work and be steady. Accordingly, I hired myself to a Mr. Geers, for a month or two. I served him faithfully, but when I wanted my pay he undertook to treat me as he would a degraded African slave. He took a cart stake in order to pay me, but he soon found out his mistake, as I made him put it down as quick as he had taken it up. I had been cheated so often that I determined to have my rights this time, and forever after.[30]

30. Apess probably reached Connecticut in the summer of 1816. This would place him in Old Hartford and New Haven in the fall and winter of 1816/17, so that his reunion with his family would have occurred in April 1817, a bit more than four years since he had run away from William Williams.

CHAPTER VIII

I was now about nineteen years of age and had become quite steady.[31] I attended meetings again quite often, and my mind was powerfully wrought upon. At this time my heart was susceptible of good impressions. I would think upon the varied scenes of my life—how often the Lord had called me, and how for a season I attended to that call—of the blessed and happy times I had experienced in the house of God, and in secret devotion—and the days of darkness and nights of sorrowful anguish since those days when the Spirit of God breathed upon my soul. *Then,* I enjoyed happiness in a preeminent degree! *Now,* I was miserable, I had offended God—violated his laws—abused his goodness—trampled his mercy underfoot and disregarded his admonitions. But still he called me back to the path of duty and of peace. I was pressed down by a load of shame and a weight of guilt too intolerable to be borne. Hour after hour, and day after day, did I endeavor to lift my heart to God, to implore forgiveness of my sins and grace to enable me to lay hold of the promise to the vilest of the vile, through Jesus Christ our Lord. But the Holy Spirit flew not to my relief. I then thought that I must die and go to hell.

My convictions were so powerful that I could scarcely eat. I had no relish for food. The anguish of my soul afflicted my body to such a degree that I was almost too weak to perform my labor. Sleep seldom visited my eyelids. My employer found out that the Lord was teaching me, but he made light of it and said he was going to heaven across the lots. I thought he might go *that* way, but for my part I must take another course.[32] May the Lord forgive him and teach him the good and the right way. By this time my employer had become good to me, and as I wished to engage elsewhere for six months, my time being out with him, he gave me a recommendation.

One of the neighbors wished me to join with him six months, so we agreed. They treated me as a brother. But my sins troubled me so much that I had no comfort. My soul was weighed down on account of my many transgressions, and I was tempted by the enemy of souls to believe that I had committed the unpardonable sin—but he was a liar, as the sequel proved, for after many prayers, and groans, and tears, and sighs, I found some relief. This, at the time, astonished me, as I was one of the vilest sinners on the face of the earth.[33] Now I think the devil took advantage of me in this manner. I

31. Spring and summer 1817.
32. To go across lots is to take a shortcut. The common saying in vernacular speech is "to go to hell across lots," precisely the implication of Apess's "I thought he might go *that* way."
33. The "unpardonable sin" is to despair of Christ's power to save one, which is, in effect, to believe oneself greater than God, to be beyond this power. To find relief signified Christ's forgiving presence and one's faith in it.

have heretofore stated that I associated with bad company, with such persons as often profaned the holy name of God. I always disliked to hear anyone swear, but one day when I was angry I swore a horrid oath, and the very instant that it passed my lips my heart beat like the pendulum of a clock, my conscience roared despair and horror like thunder, and I thought I was going to be damned right off. I gave utterance to the word without thinking what I was doing; it could not be recalled, and afterward I thought I would not have said it for all the world. This was the *first* and the *last* time that I ever used so awful an expression, and I thought this of itself sufficient to sink my soul to the shades of everlasting night. Now, the way in which the devil took the advantage of me was this: Whenever I became fervent in my supplications at the throne of mercy for pardon on my guilty soul, he would try to persuade me that I had in uttering the oath referred to forever closed the door of hope.

I still continued to pray and attend meetings, notwithstanding the work was very hard, and the meeting seven miles off; but I did not neglect attending it a single Sabbath during the summer. I generally returned, as I went, with a heavy heart. I now went to a camp meeting but did not experience that depth of enjoyment which I desired. Being determined to persevere in the way of well-doing, I united with the Methodist Society, that is, on trial, for six months. I had never been at a camp meeting and, of course, knew nothing about it. It far exceeded my expectations. I never witnessed so great a body of Christians assembled together before—I was also astonished with their proceedings, was affected by their prayers, charmed by their songs of praise, and stood gazing at them like a brainless clown. However, I soon solicited the prayers of this body of Christians, for my poor soul was greatly troubled. But behold, one of the brethren called on me to pray. I began to make excuse, but nothing would do; he said, pray, and I thought I must. I trembled through fear and began to wish myself at home; I soon got on my knees, and of all the prayers that man ever heard, this attempt must have exceeded—I feared man more than my creator God. While endeavoring to pray, it appeared as if my words would choke me—the cold chills run over my body—my feelings were indescribably awful. This, however, had a very good effect upon me, as it learned me not to please man so much as God. The camp meeting was a very happy one; I found some comfort and enjoyed myself tolerably well. The parting scene was very affecting—serious thoughts passed through my mind, as I gazed on this large number of respectable and happy people, who were about to separate and meet not together again till the blast of the archangel's trump shall bring them in a twinkling to the judgment seat of Christ. And so it was, for we have never met altogether again—some have taken their everlasting flight.

When I returned home, I began to tell the family all about the camp meeting, what a blessed time we had, etc., but they ridiculed me, saying we were only deluded. I attempted to exhort them to seek an interest in the sinner's friend, but to no purpose, as they only laughed at me.

When the time for which I engaged had expired, I went among my tribe at Groton. I lived this winter with my aunt, who was comfortably situated.[34] She was the handmaid of the Lord, and being a widow, she rented her lands to the whites, and it brought her in enough to live on. While here we had some very good times. Once in four weeks we had meeting, which was attended by people from Rhode Island, Stonington, and other places and generally lasted three days. These seasons were glorious. We observed particular forms, although we knew nothing about the dead languages, except that the knowledge thereof was not necessary for us to serve God. We had no house of divine worship, and believing "that the groves were God's first temples," thither we would repair when the weather permitted.[35] The Lord often met with us, and we were happy in spite of the devil. Whenever we separated it was in perfect love and friendship.

My aunt could not read, but she could almost preach and, in her feeble manner, endeavor to give me much instruction. Poor dear woman, her body slumbers in the grave, but her soul is in the paradise of God—she has escaped from a world of trouble. The whites were anxious to have the honor of burying her; she was interred very decently, the whites being as numerous as the natives. Indeed, all who knew her wished to show the veneration in which they held her by following her remains to their last earthly resting place. Her name was Sally George, and she was deservedly esteemed for her piety. In her sphere she was a very useful woman and greatly beloved by all who knew her. She was very attentive to the sick, kind to the unfortunate, good and benevolent to the poor and the fatherless. She would often pour into the ear of the sin-sick soul the graciously reviving promises of the Gospel. While she lay sick, she expressed a desire to go and see her brethren, who lived about eight miles off; she said the Lord would give her the strength, and so he did. She then visited her friends, and after enjoying some religious conversation, she returned home to die. The fear of death was now taken away, and she exhorted all around her to be faithful and serve the Lord. She died in the full triumphs of the faith, on the 6th of May, 1824, aged 45 years. In her death, happy as it was, the church had sustained an almost irreparable loss. But

> She bathes her weary soul,
> In seas of heavenly rest,

34. For more on Aunt Sally George, see "The Experience of Sally George" in *The Experiences of Five Christian Indians* and the introduction to this volume.
35. The line is from William Cullen Bryant's "Forest Hymn."

Where not a wave of trouble rolls,
Across her peaceful breast.[36]

The next season I engaged with a Mr. Wright in the same neighborhood and continued with him some time.[37] While there I did wrong, as I got angry at the mistress of the house, who, by the by, was an extremely passionate woman, and uttered some unguarded expressions. I found I had done wrong and instantly made my humble confession to Almighty God, and also to my brethren, and obtained forgiveness. I continued to attend meeting and had many blessed times. The spirit of the Lord moved upon my heart, and I thought it to be my duty to call sinners to repentance. It was determined to have another camp meeting this season, and Brother Hyde preached a preparatory sermon from this portion of divine truth: *By night, on my bed, I sought him whom my soul loveth: I sought him but I found him not. I will rise now, and go about the city; in the streets, and in the broad ways, I will seek him whom my soul loveth: I sought him but I found him not. The watchman that go about the city found me: to whom I said, saw ye him whom my soul loveth? It was but a little that I passed from them, but I found him whom my soul loveth: I held him and would not let him go, until I had brought him to my mother's house, and unto the chamber of her that had conceived me. I charge you, O ye daughters of Jerusalem, by the roes and by the hinds of the field, that ye stir not up, nor awake my love till he please* (Song of Solomon 3:1–5).

After Brother Hyde had concluded his sermon, I felt moved to rise and speak. I trembled at the thought; but believing it a duty required of me by my heavenly father, I could not disobey, and in rising to discharge this sacred obligation, I found all impediment of speech removed; my heart was enlarged, my soul glowed with holy fervor, and the blessing of the Almighty sanctified this, my first public attempt to warn sinners of their danger and invite them to the marriage supper of the Lamb. I was now in my proper element, just harnessed for the work, with the fire of divine love burning on my heart. In this frame of mind I went to camp meeting, and here the presence of the Lord was made manifest—his gracious spirit was poured out upon the people, and while he was present to cheer and bless his followers, his awakening power sought out the sinner and nailed conviction on his heart. Oh, it was a joyful scene. Here were the followers of the Lord praising him in strains of the liveliest joy—there the brokenhearted mourner shedding tears of penitential sorrow over the long black catalog of his offenses. Many a

---

36. This is from Isaac Watts's hymn, "When I Can Read My Title Clear."
37. Apess breaks his chronology by taking the story of Aunt Sally George through to her death. "The next season" is spring to fall 1818. He uses here, of course, the language of farming, in which a season can be planting time (spring to early summer) or harvest (late summer to midautumn) or the whole cycle of planting through harvest.

gracious shower of divine mercy fell on the encampment—many a hitherto drooping plant revived, and many a desolate and ruined heart was made the home of new, and happy, and heavenly feelings. I have reason to believe that at least one hundred sinners were reclaimed at this meeting, while many went away with their heads bowed down under a sense of their numerous transgressions. Shortly after this meeting, I felt it my duty to observe the ordinance of baptism by immersion, believing it as a scriptural doctrine. There were three other candidates for this ordinance, which was administered by Rev. Mr. Barnes, at a place called Bozrah, in the month of December 1818. It was a very solemn, affecting, and profitable time; the Lord in truth was present to bless.

Shortly after this I felt a desire to see my family connections again and therefore left this part of the country, after obtaining a certificate of my standing in society, etc., as is generally done by Methodists when they remove from one place to another. Nothing worthy of special notice occurred during my journey, except losing my way one night. It happened in this manner: Having reached the neighborhood of my father's residence about sundown, and being extremely anxious to complete my journey, I concluded to continue on, as I expected to reach his house by two o'clock in the morning. Unfortunately, I took the wrong road and was led into a swamp. I thought I was not far from the main road as I fancied that I heard teams passing on the other side of the swamp; and not being aware of the dangerous situation in which I was placed, I penetrated into the labyrinth of darkness with the hope of gaining the main road. At every step I became more and more entangled—the thickness of the branches above me shut out the little light afforded by the stars, and to my horror I found that the further I went, the deeper the mire; at last, I was brought to a dead stand. I had found it necessary to feel my way with a stick—now it failed in striking on solid ground; fortunately, in groping about I found a pole, which I suppose must have been twelve or fifteen feet long, and thrusting it in, met with no better success. I was now amazed; what to do I knew not; shut out from the light of heaven—surrounded by appalling darkness—standing on uncertain ground—and having proceeded so far that to return, if possible, were as "dangerous as to go over." This was the hour of peril—I could not call for assistance on my fellow creatures; there was no mortal ear to listen to my cry. I was shut out from the world and did not know but that I should perish there, and my fate forever remain a mystery to my friends. I raised my heart in humble prayer and supplication to the father of mercies, and behold he stretched forth his hand and delivered me from this place of danger. Shortly after I had prayed the Lord to set me free, I found a small piece of solid earth, and then another, so that after much difficulty I succeeded in once more placing my feet upon dry ground. I then fell upon my knees and thanked my blessed master for this singular interposition of his providence and mercy. As this circumstance occasioned so much delay, and withal fatigued me so much, I did not reach home until daylight. I found my father well, and all the family rejoiced to see me. On this occasion I had an opportunity of making some remarks to the friends who came to see me. My father, who was a member of the Baptist church, was much pleased, and what was far better, we had a time of refreshing from the presence of the Lord. I now agreed with my father to tarry with him all winter, and he agreed to learn me how to make shoes. In this new business I made some progress.[38]

CHAPTER IX

I was now very constant in attending meetings. In the neighborhood there was a small class of Methodists, firmly united to each other; I cast in my lot with this little band and had many precious seasons. They agreed in all points of doctrine but one, and that related to *perfect love*—some said it was inconsistent, and another said it was not.[39] I could not see wherein this inconsistency manifested itself, as we were commanded to *love God with all our hearts, and contend for that faith once delivered to the saints.*

While in Colrain the Lord moved upon my heart in a peculiarly powerful manner, and by it I was led to believe that I was called to preach the Gospel of our Lord and Savior Jesus Christ. In the present day, a great variety of opinion prevails respecting the holy work. We read in the Bible that in former days holy men spoke as they were moved by the Holy Ghost. I think this is right and believe more in the validity of such a call than in all the calls that ever issued from any body of men united.[40] My exercises were great—my soul was

38. He would have reached his father, then in Colrain, Massachusetts, sometime in the winter or early spring of 1819. A "time of refreshing" means a revival, a special outpouring of God's grace on his people. Apess did also, at this juncture, learn to be a shoemaker.

39. The argument involves the belief that Christ enjoins us to "perfect love," love like his and God the Father's, which knows no taint of self-regard and in which one is willing to lay down one's life for another. The "inconsistency" speaks to the fact that as creatures of the Fall, of original sin, we are by definition incapable of such love. Apess resolves the matter in his belief that God will make available to us what we need to meet his requirements, here signified as *"that faith once delivered to the saints."*

40. Apess addresses here one of the issues that repeatedly led to new tensions within the evangelical community under the influence of revivalism. The emphasis on inspiration and evidence of the active presence of the Holy Ghost made it difficult to defend fixed rituals of worship or forms of settled authority. One of the critical forms of authority for any institutionalized church involves the selection and discipline of its ministers. Apess positions himself with those who stress the limitations of the ways of men and the greater reliability of God's. Therefore, feeling the call to preach from within had greater authority than any examination or licensing procedure such as that employed by the Methodist Conference to decide who was qualified to preach.

pained when the Lord placed before me the depravity of human nature. I commenced searching the Scriptures more diligently, and the more I read, the more they opened to my understanding; and something said to me, "Go now and warn the people to flee from the wrath to come!" And I began immediately to confer with flesh and blood, excusing myself, saying, Lord I cannot. I was nothing but a poor ignorant Indian and thought the people would not hear me. But my mind was the more distressed, and I began to pray more frequently to God to let this "cup pass from me." In this manner was I exercised day by day; but in the evening I would find myself in our little meetings exhorting sinners to repentance and striving to comfort the saints. On these occasions I had the greatest liberty. Now I did not acquaint my brethren with my feelings or exercises, for the devil tempted me to believe that they would take no notice of it. At length, the spell that bound me was broken. I dreamt one night that I was about taking a journey, that my road lay through a miry place in a dark and dreary way. It was with no little difficulty that I descended the steep. Then I beheld at some distance before me a large plain, on which the sun shone with perfect brightness, and when I succeeded in reaching this plain, all at once an angel of the blessed Lord stood in my way. After having addressed me, he read some extracts from St. John's Gospel, respecting the preaching of the word of life. This dream was the means of troubling me still more.

I now requested, if the Lord had called me to this holy work, that he would make it manifest by a sign. So one day, after prayer, I went to a friend and told him, if he was willing to give out an appointment for meeting at his house, I would try and exhort. He assented, and in giving out the appointment he made a mistake, as he informed the people that there would be a *sermon* instead of an exhortation, and when I attended, in place of finding a few persons at my friend's house, I found a large congregation assembled at the schoolhouse. I now thought I was in a sad predicament—I had never preached; but I called mightily upon God for assistance. When I went in, every eye was fixed on me, and when I was commencing the meeting, it appeared as if my confidence in God was gone; my lips quivered, my voice trembled, my knees smote together, and in short I quaked as it were with fear. But the Lord blessed me. Some of the people were pleased, and a few displeased. Soon after this, I received an invitation to hold a meeting in the same place again. I accordingly went, and I found a great concourse of people who had come out to hear the Indian preach, and as soon as I had commenced, the sons of the devil began to show their front—and I was treated not with the greatest loving kindness, as one of them threw an old hat in my face, and this example was followed by others, who threw sticks at me. But in the midst I went on with my sermon, and spoke from 2 Peter 2:9. *The Lord knoweth how to deliver the godly out of temptations, and to reserve the unjust until the day of judgment, to be punished.* The Lord laid too his helping hand; the sons of night were confused. Now I can truly say that a native of the forest cannot be found in all our country who would not blush at the bad conduct of many who enjoy in a preeminent degree the light of the Gospel. But so it is, that in the very center of Gospel light and influence thousands of immortal souls are sitting in darkness, or walking in the valley of the shadow of death! It is the truth, and a melancholy truth indeed![41]

I had an invitation to speak at another place about nine miles distant. Still, I was not satisfied; and I made it a subject of constant and serious prayer—I implored the Lord all the way, that if I was truly called to preach the everlasting Gospel I might have some token of his favor. I found the congregation large and respectful, and I spoke from Jeremiah 6:14.[42] We had a good time, but nothing special occurred. The congregation in the afternoon was much larger than in the morning, and it was impressed upon my mind to speak from this portion of the holy Scriptures: *The Lord knoweth how to deliver the godly out of temptation, and reserve the unjust to the day of judgment to be punished.* The Lord gave me strength, and we had a most gracious and glorious exhibition of his presiding presence, as many wept bitterly on account of their sins, while the saints of the most high rejoiced in the prospect of a complete and triumphant deliverance from the power of their sworn and cruel foe. Now I was assured that my call was of God, and I returned home praising him.

Shortly after this, my father began to oppose me—perhaps he thought, with some of the whites, that there were enough preachers in the land already. Be this as it may, I continued to exercise my gift and preached wherever a door was opened and, I trust, with some success.

It was now nearly time for the Conference to commence its session, and one of our circuit preachers very kindly told me that I had better desist until I should have obtained a license; if I did not, I would break the rules of the church—but I had already violated these.[43] Considering my youth and good intentions, he overlooked this conceived error and informed me that if I waited patiently I should have a license to exercise my gift by way of exhorta-

41. Apess was now in and around Colrain in northwestern Massachusetts. His discovery of his vocation and his first exhortations would have occurred between 1819 or 1820 and the spring or summer of 1821, when he returned to Connecticut.

42. "They have healed also the hurt *of the daughter* of my people slightly, saying, Peace, peace; when *there* is no peace."

43. Quarterly Methodist Conferences controlled for particular regions all matters of discipline within the Methodist Episcopal church. The most recurrent and important had to do with who was licensed to exhort and who to preach and on what circuit, since in this period most Methodist preachers did not serve a single settled parish.

tion, and that the preacher who was to succeed him would think it wrong if he found me holding meetings without authority from my brethren, and I partly consented. But the time was so long before the matter could be finally regulated that I could not sheathe my sword, and having on the armor, I took the field and preached till the new elder come among us; and when he found me preaching, what do you think he did? Why, he placed me under censure. Now, he wanted me to confess that I was in error; but I was such a blind Indian that I could not see how I was in error in preaching *Christ Jesus, and Him crucified,* and of course could not conscientiously confess as erroneous that which I believed to be right. He told me that if I *was* right, not to confess, but as I did *not* confess he cast me out of the church, showing plainly that he believed that no person is called of God to preach his word unless ordained of man! No comment is necessary on this fact.

This unkind treatment, as I regarded it, had nearly proved the ruin of my soul. The waters of affliction had well-nigh overwhelmed me—my hopes were drowned, and having been excluded from the pales of the church, I viewed myself as an *outcast from society.* Now the enemy sought to prevail against me, and for a season overcome me; I gave way for a little while but soon returned to my *first love.* I went then to my native tribe, where meetings were still kept up. I tarried here but a short time and then went to Old Saybrook; here I found a few Methodists, but they were too feeble to form a society, as persecution was at its height.[44] There were also a few colored people who met regularly for religious worship; with these I sometimes assembled.

About this time I met with a woman of nearly the same color as myself— she bore a pious and exemplary character.[45] After a short acquaintance, we were united in the sacred bonds of marriage; and now I was going on prosperously; but at last a calamity fell upon me, which nearly crushed me to the dust. A man exacted work of me, for a debt that I did not honestly owe, and while making his shoes, I concluded to pay myself, which I did. Immediately my conscience smote me, but I could not replace it in time, so I made ample restitution and a frank confession before all my brethren—and the Lord was good, for he wiped out the blot and restored me to his favor. I then went to Middletown and remained a short time, where I got out of business;

44. It appears he left the area around Colrain and returned to southeastern Connecticut sometime between late winter and spring 1820/21.

45. This would have occurred in the fall of 1821 since William Apess and Mary Wood of Salem, Connecticut, were married in that town on December 16, 1821, by the Reverend John Whittlesey. Mary Wood's mother, by her account, was an "English woman," and her father from one of the Spanish islands. He was, it would seem, of either mixed Native and Hispanic American ancestry or African and Hispanic or possibly all three.

crossed over the river and agreed to serve a tavern keeper for one month. I
now sought every opportunity to be alone, and when my month was up I
received my wages and sent it to my wife. I had now to seek another place, and
as I went along, I prayed that my family might not suffer, as I knew that they
were innocent, and my little ones too small to help themselves. After a little
while, the Lord opened the way, and I obtained a situation with a Mr. Hail, in
Gloucester, for two months, at twelve dollars a month. It being harvest time,
my employer allowed each of his hands a half-pint of spirits every day. I told
him I did not want my portion, so he agreed to pay me a little more. I *abstained
entirely, and found that I could not only stand labor as well but perform more than those
who drank the spirits.* All the hands exclaimed against me and said that I would
soon give out; but I was determined that *touch not, taste not, handle not,* should
be my motto; God supported me, and I can truly say that my health was
better, my appetite improved, and my mind was calm. My general drink was
molasses, or milk and water. Some persons say, that *they* cannot do without
spirituous liquors, but I say it is a curse to individuals, to families, to communities, to the nation, and to the world at large. I could enlarge on this
momentous subject—I could speak from experience, as I have too often felt
its baneful effects, but as I intend, if the Lord spares me, to publish an essay on
Intemperance, I leave it for the present. When my time was out, Mr. Hail paid
me like a gentleman and also gave me three dollars and twenty-five cents, in
lieu of the spirits—a sum sufficient to buy my poor dear children some
clothes. The family were loath to part with me, as I had endeavored to live a
godly life—I held a prayer meeting with them and departed with tears in
my eyes.

I now bent my course for Hartford and engaged labor work at twenty
dollars a month—then I went home and spent one week with my dear family
and, according to my engagements, returned to Hartford, but my place was
taken up, and I did not know what to do. While in this extremity, a thought
struck me—I remembered that I had a sister living in Providence. Thither I
went and soon found my sister, who was very kind to me. I had no difficulty in
procuring work.[46] The Spirit of the Lord now fell afresh upon me, and I at
once entered into the work without conferring with flesh and blood. I appointed meeting for exhortation and prayer—the Lord blessed my feeble
efforts, and souls were converted and added to the church. I continued here

46. Apess's separation from his family and constant journeying in search of work characterized the
necessities affecting not only most Native Americans in New England but many, if not most,
propertyless Americans for much of the nineteenth century. He would have gone to Providence
the first time sometime circa 1825/26, I think—given his reference to several children. The sister
was probably Mary Ann (b. ca. 1805). She was married twice—first to a Peters and then to Anthony
Tattoon.

five months and then, taking a letter of recommendation, returned to my family; and when I had concluded to remove to Providence, as the place of my future residence, the society gave me a certificate to the church in Providence—I there joined, and I was shortly appointed to the office of class leader, which office I filled for two years.[47] I now obtained a verbal permission to appoint meetings from Brother Webb, the preacher in charge. Brother Kent succeeded him. After this change I applied for a license to exhort—but I was opposed by two or three persons on account of not having lived long enough in the place. The rest of the class, about thirty in number, were anxious that I should have a license, and a division had like to have been the consequence of withholding it from me. In a month or two after, the affair was settled to mutual satisfaction, and it was agreed that I should have license to exhort. I went from place to place, improving my gift, and the Lord blessed my labors. I now felt it more strongly my duty, and an inward satisfaction in preaching the "word." Sometimes, however, the evil one would tempt me to give it up, but instantly my conscience would reprove me. Many a severe combat have I had with the enemy respecting my competency, and I come to the conclusion that if I could not give *"refined!"* instruction, and neglected to discharge my duty to God and my fellow men on that account, I could not enjoy his smiles. So I was determined in the strength of the Lord to go on in the way wherein I was called.

My mind was now exercised about entering the work as a missionary. I prayed to the Lord, if it was his will to open the way, as I was poor, and had a family to maintain, and did not wish to depend upon public charity. My desire was to do something at the same time that would enable me to keep my family. Now, a gentleman wished me to take out some religious books and sell them. I did so and went praying to God all the way to bless me—and so he did, and his blessing attended my labors wherever I went. I had also some success in selling my books and made enough to support my little family and defray my necessary traveling expenses. So I concluded to travel, and the Lord went with me. In one of these excursions, I went over on Long Island and from thence to New York, where my bodily strength was reduced by a fever. Here in the hour of sickness the Lord was with me—I experienced his comforting presence, the kindness of friends, and the quiet of a peaceful conscience. It was a sore trial for me to be absent, in such a situation, from my family, but it "was good to be afflicted"—and how beautiful was this passage of Scripture fulfilled which says, *Seek first the kingdom of heaven, and all things else shall be added.* How beautiful and numerous are his promises, and how strikingly fulfilled. I

---

47. The Methodists organized themselves locally into societies, which were in turn divided into smaller groups, "classes," for purposes of prayer and exhortation.

have seen all these promises verified. Blessings unnumbered and undeserved showered upon me.

From New York I went to Albany, stopping at the different villages and exhorting the people to repentance, and the Lord seconded my efforts. I was very sick for about one month, and my friends thought I would not recover; but although I was very much reduced, I did not think my sands had yet run their course—I believed that God would spare me to preach his Gospel; and according to my faith it was, for I speedily recovered and commenced again my labor of love. On Arbor Hill the Lord poured out his spirit in a powerful manner. Here a class of about thirty members was organized, and at a number of places where I labored several were added, but how many in the whole I cannot say precisely; let it suffice that through my instrumentality some souls were brought from a state of sin and darkness to the light and favor of God— to whom be all the glory ascribed.

After having been absent six months I returned home and found my dear family and friends in the enjoyment of their usual health. After remaining about a fortnight, I went to Boston. Here the Lord blessed my labors among the friends of the cross. While in Boston I met with a professed infidel, who wished to draw me into an argument by hooting at me for believing in Jesus Christ, the Savior of fallen men. I spoke to him about being a *good gentleman,* and he replied that I, in common with my brethren, believed that no man was a gentleman unless he was under the influence of priestcraft; and I told him that I considered every man a gentleman who acted in a becoming manner. He then asked by what authority I believed in Jesus Christ as my Savior; I answered, by an internal witness in my soul, and the enjoyment of *that* peace emanating from this Savior, which the "world can neither give nor take away." This stirred his passions, and he said, "I suppose you think I am an atheist," to which I replied in the negative and assured him that he was an infidel.[48] I then spoke to him of Jesus Christ and his Apostles; and he replied that they were all fools together and I was as great a one as any. He turned pale and looked as if he would have swallowed me up alive—and I gave him an exhortation and went on my way. After spending about two months in Boston, I returned home; then I visited New Bedford, Martha's Vineyard, and Nantucket, preaching the word wherever a door was opened—and the Lord was not unmindful of me, his presence accompanied me, and I believe that much good was done. Again I visited my family and then went to Salem, and I found many precious souls. We held several meetings, and the Lord came forth in the galleries of grace, and my labor of love proved very profit-

48. The distinction is a fine one. An atheist is anyone who denies the existence of God, or gods. An infidel is someone who specifically rejects Christianity and is actively hostile to it.

able to the dear people, and when I left them the parting scene was very affecting. I now visited the different towns, preaching as I went along, until I reached Newburyport, and having taken letters of recommendation from the various preachers, I was kindly received; and reporting myself to Brother Bartholomew Otheman, the preacher in charge, he provided lodgings for me. It so happened that Brother John Foster, his colleague, was sick, and they needed some help, and I thought the brethren were glad that I had come among them. At night I preached for Brother Otheman, and the next evening in the church where Brother Foster officiated, and an appointment was given out for me to preach in the course of the next Sunday at the same church, but having an intercourse in the meantime with Brother Foster, and finding him highly tinctured with Calvinism, I thought I would converse freely with him on the subject.[49] This course soured his mind against me, and he gave out my future appointments in such a way that I thought best to preach the word in the dwelling houses of the inhabitants; and I had as many hearers as I could have wished, and I bless the Lord that much good was done in his name. I made several attempts toward a reconciliation; he could hear no proposals, I could make no concessions, as I had not injured or given him any cause of offense; and he went on to persecute me, notwithstanding the remonstrances of his brethren. My motives were pure, and I bless the Lord that a day will come when the secrets of all hearts shall be revealed. I forgive the poor man for all the injury he attempted to do me, and I hope the righteous judge of all men will also forgive him.

From Newburyport I went to Portland, Maine, where I had some gracious times and labored with success, and then returned to my abiding place at Providence, R.I., with a recommendation. I reported myself to the preacher in charge and asked for a certificate; he said that my recommendation was "genuine," but he had heard evil reports respecting me and preferred inquiring into the matter before he granted my request. I felt glad that the brother had promised to make inquiry, as I knew that I should come out well. As this would take some time I crossed over to Long Island, preached at Sag Harbor and other places with success, and then went to New York, where I remained but a short time and then proceeded to Albany. Here I was known and was received in a friendly way and continued to preach wherever an opportunity offered; while here, a certificate of my membership was received from the church in Providence, and on the force of it I entered the church. I now applied for license to preach and was recommended to the quarterly

49. Brother Foster, this is to say, doubted the ability of people to come to Christ by their own efforts and will.

Conference as a suitable candidate, but the Conference thought differently; so after improving my gift three months I made another application.[50]

I had been advised by the preachers to improve on Watervliet circuit in order that they might have an opportunity to form an estimate of my talents and usefulness, and this was right. I accordingly went forward with fear and trembling, but the Lord enabled me to take up the cross and stood by me at this time. Several, I trust, through my instrumentality, passed from death unto life. I held meetings in Albany, and crowds flocked out, some to *hear* the truth and others to *see* the "Indian." The worth of souls lay near my heart, and the Lord was pleased to own the labors of his feeble servant. From Albany I went to Bath, where the power of the Almighty was felt in a wonderful manner; it appeared as though all the inhabitants were engaged in seeking the salvation of their souls—many wept bitterly and cried aloud for mercy, and seven or eight in the judgment of charity *passed from death unto life.* I then went on to my appointment at Watervliet, and here the Lord was present to awaken sinners and reclaim backsliders.

At Troy I found a number of good Christian friends, with whom I had several very good meetings, and the power of the Lord was made manifest. One evening as I was preaching to some colored people, in a schoolhouse, the power of the Lord moved on the congregation, both white and colored—hard hearts began to melt and inquire what they must do to be saved. We had a very *refreshing season from the presence of the Lord.*

I now went into all surrounding villages preaching the word of eternal life and exhorting sinners to repentance. Before the quarterly meeting, I took a tour to the west, as far as Utica, holding meetings by the way, and I found God as precious as ever; and being absent three weeks, I returned in order to attend the Conference, which was to be held on the 11th of April.[51]

I can truly say that the spirit of prejudice is no longer an inmate of my bosom; the sun of consolation has warmed my heart, and by the grace of God assisting me, I am determined to sound the trump of the Gospel—to call upon men to turn and live. Look, brethren, at the natives of the forest—they come, notwithstanding you call them "*savage,*" from the "east and from the west, the north and the south," and will occupy seats in the kingdom of heaven before you. Let us one and all "contend" valiantly "for that faith once

---

50. At this point Apess cut out nearly eight pages from the first edition. These narrate his conflict with the Conference of the Methodist Episcopal church over the right to preach and his conviction that he was being denied ordination because he was an Indian. He leaves the Methodist Episcopals and joins the newly forming antiepiscopal Protestant Methodist church, which ordains him in 1829/30. These passages are printed in their entirety in the Textual Note below.

51. 1829.

delivered to the saints"; and if we are contented, and love God with all our hearts, and desire the enjoyment of his peaceful presence, we shall be able to say with the poet,

> Let others stretch their arms like seas,
> And grasp in all the shore;
> Grant me the visits of his grace,
> And I desire no more.[52]

Now, my dear reader, I have endeavored to give you a short but correct statement of the leading features of my life. When I think of what I am, and how wonderfully the Lord has led me, I am dumb before him. When I contrast my situation with that of the rest of my family, and many of my tribe, I am led to adore the goodness of God. When I reflect upon my many misdeeds and wanderings, and the dangers to which I was consequently exposed, I am lost in astonishment at the long forbearance and the unmerited mercy of God. I stand before you as a monument of his unfailing goodness. May that same mercy which has upheld me still be my portion—and may author and reader be preserved until the perfect day and dwell forever in the paradise of God.

William Apess

TEXTUAL NOTE

The paragraphs below provide the most important material Apess cut from the 1829 edition of *A Son of the Forest* when he revised it for the 1831 edition. They are included here for their historical and biographical value and keyed to the chapter, page, and paragraph in this edition.

IX: 50, #1. At the end of this paragraph begin the major cuts from the 1829 edition: "But before I proceed to narrate the doings of the conference, I will inform the reader what the Lord did for me in the mean time." This excision signals the entire omission of Apess's experience with the Conference in Albany, New York, in April 1829.

IX: 51, #1. After the paragraph about his success in Watervliet in awakening sinners and reclaiming backsliders, the following has been removed: "My wife and my little son had taken board with one of the brethren. About this time I left the circuit for a spell, as I had some business at Hudson which I had to transact in person, and I felt no uneasiness about my family, presuming that they would be made comfortable as I paid for their board. On my return, I found my wife quite unwell—and I pretty soon learned that the treatment she received was

---

52. Another Isaac Watts hymn, "God, My Only Happiness."

very unkind, if not cruel — not fit for a dog, and what surprised me was that the woman of the house where my poor wife was boarded, and who treated her so bad, *professed* to be a Methodist. She was even so cruel as to refuse a light in her room, and when medicines were ordered, she had to take them without sweetening, or anything whatsoever to make them palatable. No wonder, therefore, that on my return, I found my wife dissatisfied with her situation and anxious for a change. But she was unwell, and I endeavored to pacify her, believing it improper to remove her at that season, on account of the deep snow and intense cold. So we concluded to stay a little longer and I purchased some few necessaries for my wife. However we soon moved to Troy, in order to get out of such an unlucky dilemma; my wife was extremely rejoiced to get out of their fangs."

IX: 51, #3. After this paragraph in the 1829 comes the entire account of what happened at the April Conference and after. There is no trace of it in the 1831 edition; indeed there is no mention that he left the Methodist Episcopal church to join the newly forming Protestant Methodist church which would and did ordain him sometime later in 1829 or early in 1830: "At the time appointed the meeting was held. A preparatory sermon was preached by the presiding elder — the conference was called, and the business of the circuit was attended to. My case came up in course, and the president (the P[residing] E[lder]) asked me if I thought the Lord had called me to preach, to which I answered in the affirmative. I was then questioned as to my faith in the doctrine and discipline of the church, and whether I would conform to the same, to which I assented. An opportunity was now given to the brethren to ask me any questions they thought proper; one only was asked, and that was, how long I had been converted. I then withdrew from the room to give them an opportunity to decide on my application. My mind was perfectly easy. After I was out about half an hour, Brother Strong came out to inform me that the conference would rather that I should take an exhorter's license again, as they knew nothing of my character, but all the while they knew nothing against me. Now let it be observed that I had not only presented a certificate of my good standing, but also a number of recommendations of character and usefulness, from several well-known itinerant ministers of the connection, and as they could find nothing against me, it appeared singular to me, that men who had thrown open their doors to the poor Indian, and had often sat with apparent profit under his ministry, could thus oppose me, and cry out 'We do not know you.' I told the brother who gave me this information that if they did not comply, that they would hinder my doing that work which the Lord required of me. He then returned, and after deliberating about fifteen minutes, I was called in, when the presiding elder (Stratton) said. 'This conference does not see fit to grant your request — are you willing to receive an exhorter's license again?' To which I hastily replied in the negative. After considering the subject a little, I spoke to Brother Covel, the preacher in charge, and he advised me to take an exhorter's relation: *a license was readily granted me to exhort.* Now, one single question which I will leave with the reader to answer, viz: As this conference refused me a license to preach on the ground that its members did not know enough of my character, had they any right to grant a license to exhort, at the *same time* that they refused one to preach?

"Shortly after, I met Brother Covel and his colleague in Albany and informed them that it was my intention not to present the papers I had received to the *Episcopal Methodists,* as it was my intention to join the *Methodist Society.* They appeared somewhat surprised and endeavored to persuade me to remain where I was, that is, not to leave the church. I told them that my mind was fully made up — there was too much oppression for me in the old church, and that a disposition prevailed to keep the local preachers down. They then asked me why I had said that I believed in the doctrine and discipline. — I replied that I did fully believe in the *doctrine,* but that I had taken exceptions to the *discipline*; that while I was with them and they did not stretch the chords of government too tight, I was contented, but I could not go the whole, and pin my faith and hope, as many of them did, entirely upon their government. They appeared to think that I had done wrong in saying that I would be governed by the discipline — but I could not see in the same glass, for as long as I continued in *that* church I conformed to *its* rules; and as this law was not continuous in its nature, whenever I ceased to be a member of that church, its binding and distinctive law, touching my *person* and my conduct became *dead* — it had no farther of future jurisdiction over me. I cannot think that I violated any holy law, by promising obedience to the rules of the Methodist Episcopal Church, and redeeming that pledge so long as I continued in the jurisdiction of its law. But I will tell the reader that in the judgment of charity, I think they (the members of the conference) broke the commandments of God; Brother Covel said, 'As it has come to this, I will tell you that it was mentioned (much to your prejudice in the conference) that your wife in a *hasty way,* or unguarded moment, had said that she would expose you.' Now this had a bad appearance — the term of itself is bad enough, as it implies guilt, or offense of some kind — and this slang was retailed and descanted on in the conference, and what do you think they did with it? — It was raised as a barrier between me and a license from *men* professedly religious to preach the Gospel; and I should never have known the cause if I had not left the church!!! I told Brother Covel that I could not believe my wife had ever said it, and on asking her she had no recollection of saying any such thing, and I believe her. I ascertained that the report came from the woman who was so cruel to my wife, while I was absent at Hudson, as related before, she was angry with us, and sought, I think, to do us evil. Should not the members of the conference have informed me of this circumstance, and by neglecting to do so, did they not violate the command-ment of God, which says explicitly, " 'If thou hast ought against thy brother, go and be reconciled to thy brother!' I presume that every candid reader will say, if they credit my statement, that they violated this sacred and imperative obliga-tion.

"I will not charge this to the members of the church at large, and condemn *all* for the unkind and improper conduct of a *few*. Far be such a course from me. If their life corresponds with the Gospel, I can take them by the hand, and I hope they may all contend for that faith which *was once delivered to the saints;* and wherever I see the image of Christ, there I can [find] fellowship — and where my lot is now cast I think I can be more useful in promoting the glory of God. It is a great trial for me to be [a] *mouth for God* — to stand up before my fellow men, and warn them to flee the wrath to come. I do it to please God and not man, from a settled conviction that it is my duty, and that I cannot remain in the enjoyment of religion if I neglect it.

"I pray God to banish all prejudice from my mind — that it may die forever should be the prayer of every person; but I suspect that this will not be the case with many of my brethren in the Methodist Episcopal Church — they do not like this separation which is contrary to their former sayings, for when I joined them, it was on the express condition that I should stay with them as long as I liked them — and I did so. I have frequently heard them say, when a member was dissatisfied, or could enjoy himself better elsewhere, that they would hold up both hands for him to go — but let him go and join another church, and what a storm they will raise; and in fact, they had rather that those who leave them should remain without the pales of any church rather than join the Methodist Society. It is greatly to be lamented that a spirit like this is felt, and exhibited. I feel a great deal happier in the *new* than I did in the *old* church — the govern-ment of the first is founded on *republican*, while that of the latter is founded on *monarchial* principles — and surely in this land where the tree of liberty has been nourished by the blood of thousands, we have good cause to contend for *mutual rights,* more especially as the Lord himself *died to make us free!* I rejoice sincerely in the spread of the principles of civil and religious liberty — may they ever be found 'hand in hand' accomplishing the designs of God, in promoting the welfare of mankind. If these blessed principles prevail, sectarianism will lose its influence, and the image of God in his members will be a sufficient passport to all Christian privileges; and all the followers of the most high will unite together in singing the song of praise, 'Glory to God in the highest,' etc."

The issues at play here can only seem obscure to most readers in the twentieth century. The American Methodists, in 1784, earlier than all other denominations, organized themselves into a national entity. The spread of revivalism, especially its great stirring up on the western frontier in 1797 with the Second Great Awakening, fostered within all the established churches great impatience with any form of hierarchical authority. Many wished to approximate what they believed was the egalitarian organization of the early Christian communities. As a result, schisms and splits of every kind occurred within every denomination. To these the Methodists were perhaps no more vulnerable than others, but from early in the nineteenth century many of its members chafed against the rule of bishops and the authority of the Conference. These agitations were at their height at exactly the time Apess found his vocation as a preacher. A number of Methodist preachers were expelled from the church in the 1820s, a large enough number to begin to form new and, initially, entirely locally based Methodist societies. The Methodist Episcopals were, then, especially sensitive about preachers who showed signs of disregarding the settled forms of authority. A number of times before he requested a license to preach, Apess had simply ignored the rules, and it was, I suspect, for this reason that the Conference refused his request and asked him to wait longer. His account suggests his awareness that this was probably the cause; however, his story about his wife's being abused by the woman in the lodging house and his reminders to the reader of his status as an Indian also indicate that he suspected, or wanted his readers to do so, that the denial of his request for a license to preach might have been simply one more expression of white racism. The various Methodist societies which had formed in opposition to the Methodist Episcopal hierarchy united in 1830 under the name of the Protestant Methodists and it was to this new denomination that Apess joined himself.

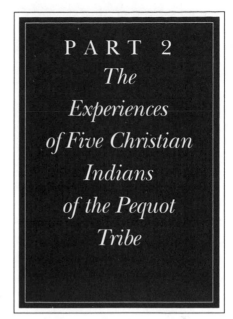

PART 2

The Experiences of Five Christian Indians of the Pequot Tribe

The Experiences of Five Christian Indians of the Pequot Tribe (1833) may be, in its first edition, the most artfully constructed of Apess's books. The narration of his own life, which opens the book, articulates an almost unqualified condemnation of white people for what they have done to the natives of the continent. In form an account of his conversion, it is in effect an exploration of the barriers to achieving an affirmative identity as a Native American in the eastern United States in the first third of the nineteenth century.

The five conversion accounts which make up the main body of the book can be read as a variation on this theme, though in each of them the discovery that Christianity can be a faith open to all people is formative. With the important exception of Aunt Sally George, all of these people were effectively orphans and either raised in the households of whites or economically bound to them by other means. But for Aunt Sally, all of them can achieve a Christian faith only by overcoming not only the indifference of most whites to the state of Indian souls but also the unapologetic racism practiced by white professors of Christianity. How could an Indian espouse a faith which itself was used to justify his or her oppression? Hannah Caleb strikes this note, which recurs throughout the book: "the poor Indians, the poor Indians, the people to whom I was wedded by the common ties of nature, were set at naught by those professors of grace, merely because we were Indians." The power of Christian faith, then, is shown to be manifested not in whites but in each of these converts, who are, with it, able to overcome the enmity they feel toward white people and love them despite the absence of any reciprocation.

The life of Aunt Sally George is situated so as to heighten the impact of the critique of whites and of their limited grasp of the religion by which they mean to justify their claims to superiority over Native Americans. Her saintliness impresses itself in no small measure through Apess's reiteration that she was regarded as holy by all who encountered her, white people and Indians. She becomes almost luminous in the text in her power to overcome what the reader has come to understand as the nearly insuperable blindness and hypocrisy of white Christians. Though her account lacks the overt critique of the others, it, too, indicates the personal devastation of being a member of a despised and subordinated group. The conversion crisis in Aunt Sally George's life involves her decision to take her own life when she was a young woman and her being lifted by her prayers to Christ. She does not explain what moved her despair, but at this point in the book a reader needs no elaboration.

The placement of the final conversion account, Anne Wampy's, suggests the subtlety of Apess's grasp of Euro-Americans' images of Indians. Anne Wampy is a drunk, a basket maker, old and poverty-stricken, without children, as clearly at the end of the line as one might get. Only the intensity of her hatred of white people might modulate these enclosing stereotypes. Her conversion near the end of her life becomes, however, not a rejection of Indian ways but an overcoming of the oppression of white people, which she has internalized.

"Conversion," which for most white readers would conventionally have read as a synonym for assimilation, becomes the medium, instead, for an affirmation of Indian pride and autonomy. And whites, not Indians, become those in need of conversion. By expropriating the very language of white justification and turning it back upon them, Apess also engages in a linguistic conversion. His deliberate reversals of the vocabulary of subordination become explicit in the concluding essay, "An Indian's Looking-Glass for the White Man." Christ as a Jew is recalled as a man of color and whites as the most degraded people in his day. Those in need of conversion become the white "civilizers"; the true Christians, by both heritage and practice, become Native Americans: "If you can find a spirit like Jesus Christ and his Apostles prevailing now in any of the white congregations, I should like to know it."

THE EXPERIENCE OF THE MISSIONARY

It is not my intention to descend to particulars in this pamphlet, any farther than to notice the origin of my life for the purpose of giving the youth a transient view between their condition and mine; or those poor children of the forest, who have had taken from them their once delightful plains and homes of their peaceful habitations; their fathers and mothers torn from their dwellings, and they left to mourn, and drop a tear, and die, over the ruins of their ancient sires. Perhaps you may ask, Why is this? I answer, because of deception and power, assisted with the fiery waters of the earth—rum. Such, my young friends, was the case of this poor self-taught Indian youth, whose experiences you are about to read.

My parentage, according to the custom of the country, was none of the least—being the descendant of a chief, or the head officer of the nation. But this availed nothing with me; the land of my fathers was gone; and their characters were not known as human beings but as beasts of prey. We were represented as having no souls to save, or to lose, but as partridges upon the mountains. All these degrading titles were heaped upon us. Thus, you see, we had to bear all this tide of degradation, while prejudice stung every white man, from the oldest to the youngest, to the very center of the heart.

It was thought no crime for old and young to hiss at the poor Indians, the noblest work of God, who had met with great misfortunes, and lost everything they had, by those very persons who despised them; yea, look which way they would, they could see no friends, nor even hear a pleasant sound from the lips of the white. Yea, there was but little help for them.

When you read this, ask yourselves if ever you had such trials. If not, begin now to prize your privileges and show pity to those whose fates are wretched and cruel. I shall now enter more fully upon my experience in childhood. It will be well to speak to the point; I shall make but few remarks here, as I intend publishing, should the Lord spare my life, a book of 300 pages, 18 mo. in size; and there the reader will find particulars respecting my life.[1]

My parents were of the same disposition of the Indians, that is, to wander to and fro. And, although my father was partly white, yet he had so much of the native blood that he fashioned after them in traveling from river to river, and from mountain to mountain, and plain to plain, on their journey.

I was born at Colrain, Massachusetts, A.D. 1798, on the 30th day of January.[2] We lived here but a few months and then removed to Colchester, Connecticut, within about twelve miles of our native tribe; and there, to my sad misfortune, my father and mother parted, I being at this time but a babe, being not more than three years old, and I saw my mother's face no more for twenty years. I was then placed with my grandparents on my mother's side, who, my readers, were not the best people in the world: for they would at times drink New England rum, and then I was neglected. How awful it is to have parents who will drink spirituous liquors or alcohol and, by that, to neglect their dear little children and leave them to suffer. You will see how much I had to suffer on the account of rum.

During my stay with the old folks our fare was hard, there being five children of us, and our fare was about equal as to earthly comforts. Sometimes we had something to eat, and at other times nothing. Many are the times in which we have gone to bed supperless, to rest our little weary limbs, stretched upon a bundle of straw, and how thankful we were for this comfort; and in the morning we were thankful to get a cold potato for our breakfasts. We thought it good fare. There was a white man who lived about a mile off, and he would, at times, bring us some frozen milk, which for a time supplied the calls of nature. We suffered thus from the cold; the calls of nature, as with almost nakedness; and calumny heaped upon us by the whites to an intense degree.

Little children, how thankful you ought to be that you are not in the same condition that we were, that you have not a nation to hiss at you, merely because your skins are white. I am sure that I rejoice for you, that it is not the case. But to proceed: At a certain time, when my grandmother had been out among the whites, with her baskets and brooms, and had fomented herself with the fiery waters of the earth, so that she had lost her reason and judgment and, in this fit of intoxication, raged most bitterly and in the meantime fell to beating me most cruelly; calling for whips, at the same time, of unnatural size, to beat me with; and asking me, at the same time, question after

1. This seems unambiguously a reference to *A Son of the Forest*, not to an entirely new and second autobiography, and thus suggests that some, if not most, of "The Experience of the Missionary" was drafted before the writing of *A Son of the Forest* in 1828/29.

2. January 31 is the date he gives in *A Son of the Forest*.

question, if I hated her. And I would say yes at every question; and the reason why was because I knew no other form of words. Thus I was beaten, until my poor little body was mangled and my little arm broken into three pieces, and in this horrible situation left for a while. And had it not been for an uncle of mine, who lived in the other part of the old hut, I think that she would have finished my days; but through the goodness of God, I was snatched from an untimely grave.

The white man will say, "What cruel creatures, to use children so!" If I could see that this blame was attached to the poor degraded Indians, I should not have one word to say. But when not a whit of it belongs to them, I have the more to say. My sufferings certainly were through the white man's measure; for they most certainly brought spirituous liquors first among my people. For surely no such sufferings were heard of, or known among our people, until the burning curse and demon of despair came among us: Surely it came through the hands of the whites. Surely the red man had never sought to destroy one another as this bane of hell would! And we little babes of the forest had to suffer much on its account. Oh white man! How can you account to God for this? Are you not afraid that the children of the forest will rise up in judgment and condemn you?

Little children, if you have parents that drink the fiery waters, do all you can, both by your tears and prayers and friendly admonitions, to persuade them to stop; for it will most certainly ruin them, if they persist in it. But to proceed: I did not long continue in this situation but was relieved from it by my uncle making his complaint to the selectmen of the town, who took up my case and placed me for a while among some of the white neighbors, until I was healed of my wounds, although it was a year before I was able to help myself much without aid. Being now about five or six years old, it was agreed upon that I should live with this white family until I had arrived at the age of twenty-one. They, being Baptist people and having no children of their own, became more fond of me than is usual for people to be of adopted children and treated me with the utmost kindness, and particularly Mrs. Furman, who was very kind and generous. And as they had agreed to send me to school, accordingly, when I had arrived at the age of six years, they sent me to school. And this they continued to do for six successive winters, which was about all the education that I received. The amount of benefit which I have received from this, none can tell. To God be all the praise.

Things began now to wear a different aspect; and my little heart began again to be expanded, and I began to be inquisitive about many things. At times, the children of God would assemble around me, to worship the Great Spirit, something new to me. Of course I listened with great attention. Their songs were sweet, and as the oil of joy no doubt was in their hearts to indite their petitions, to nerve their admonitions, to send home the word to the hearts of those who heard it, doubtless made it the more interesting. And so it caught my youthful heart, being a constant hearer of these things. And my mind became more knitted together with them. And I would question Mrs. Furman respecting these things. She would give me a great many good, wholesome admonitions and tell me the young must die as well the old, and often point me to the graveyard and cite me to small graves and warn me to prepare to die. It would leave a powerful effect upon my mind, which was not easily effaced. I recollect the first time I visited a chapel for the worship of God. It being a new place, and looking to me somewhat fine to the eye, I took great liberties, was something like a country clown passing through populous villages and cities, staring all the while upon those fine piles of buildings which he saw, or like a rabble of boys and girls going to church to hear the Indian preach: something so indeed, and so much so that I lost my balance of behavior. And when I returned I received a short address, accompanied with a handsome present, that I have not yet forgotten; it weighed well with me, so that forever afterward I was enabled to keep my balance well. It would be well for heads of families to supply their children with such presents, when needed; it would save the country from much disgrace. But to proceed: When I was about eight years old, the preaching of the Gospel powerfully affected my mind, although I was ignorant of the plan of salvation through Jesus Christ; but I had no doubt but the word was spoken with divine authority, which not only drew tears of contrition from *me* but from many others. But being small, and of little note in the world, no one supposed that I wanted religion.

In those days, the aged thought the youth were not subjects of grace; such is the fact, although it may be surprising to many; so there was none to comfort the little Indian boy. How different now! Lord, help the youth who are exalted to heaven in point of privileges so to prize them, that they might not be thrust down to hell.

I would remark here that many rise up against this doctrine; but why not rise up against, or in opposition to, the state's prison and house of correction and even the gallows itself? These are places to punish the people for their crimes. Some say their crimes are punished here; indeed, this is a new doctrine. Whoever saw a crime in the state's prison, locked up to hard labor; or whoever saw a crime hung up by the neck? How absurd, then, to delineate such doctrine. Crime is crime and stands for what is, let scoffers say what they will; may grace be imparted to enlighten our eyes. But to return: For the profiting of the youth, I would speak a little further of the exercises of my mind. Although they could not believe that I wanted religion, yet the Spirit of the Lord followed me daily; and my mind was so overwhelmed that I could hardly contain myself to rest without giving vent to my feelings. But little did the people with whom I lived think that I was serious about a future state; and although I could weep to be at church, yet they would deny me at times, saying I only wanted to look at the boys and play with them. Those sudden rebuffs would dampen my serious thoughts, and I would turn away to wicked paths of vice and unite with wicked boys and break the Sabbath, by wandering to and fro about the swamps, hedges, ponds, and brooks, sporting with whatever came in our way. But when I came home at night and retired to rest, the darkness itself was a terror to me, as I would picture to my imagination that the fiends of night stood around me, ready to devour me. Then I would cry to the Lord to have mercy upon my poor soul and promise him, if he would spare me, I would do better. But, when the darkness was past, I, like Pharaoh, forgot my promise: Thus I was led on by wicked youths until I was almost ruined, until I was persuaded to leave my home and wander to and fro to seek my bread. This displeased Mr. Furman; he, supposing I had become discontented, had sought me out another place, without my consent, which displeased me and made me more discontented than ever, I being at this time about ten years of age, entirely unfit to choose for myself. But so it was; I was alone in the world, fatherless, motherless, and helpless, as it were, and none to speak for the poor little Indian boy. Had my skin been white, with the same abilities and the same parentage, there could not have been found a place good enough for me. But such is the case with depraved nature, that their judgment for fancy only sets upon the eye, skin, nose, lips, cheeks, chin, or teeth and, sometimes, the forehead and hair; without any further examination, the mind is made up and the price set. This is something like buying chaff for wheat, or twigs of wood for solid substance.

But to proceed with our story: The place that he had procured for me was with a people professing religion that belonged to the Presbyterian church, and withal very strict. They also thought much of themselves, he being formerly a judge, likewise a member of Congress, in the House of Representatives, and had sufficient to supply all the common calls of life, for all his household.[3] I went to try my new home; and while there on trial, they used me pretty fairly, made me a few presents suited to please children, etc. They had now secured my favor, as they thought; the agreement was now made that I should have clothing and schooling, so as to read and write, and plenty of work. Now this man is what is generally called an enlightened Christian.

But let us look at his proceedings and see if he was actuated by the spirit of Christ or the custom of the day: Hear, and then decide. And there was work

3. Judge Hillhouse in fact sat in the Continental Congress, never the House of Representatives.

enough. This part of the bargain was completely fulfilled on his part, and that was all. As to my fare, it was none of the best, though middling: It was not so bad as I have seen—I mean my table fare and lodging—but when we came to the clothing part, it was mean enough, I can assure you. I was not fit to be seen anywhere among decent folks, and of course there was no meeting for me to attend, although I had a desire. But this good man did not care much about the Indian boy. He wished to hear me read: I could make out to spell a few words, and the judge said, "You are a good reader." I hope he was a better judge at law. Now, some may think me hard, but truth will stand.

Now, the judge had family prayers and was exact in having all his family to hear him pray; so he would always have a repetition of words, and I soon could pray as well as he; and of course I did not care for his prayers any longer. I would remark, however, that a colored woman, who had lived with the judge for many years, told me that he once prayed, though previous to it there was one of the most powerful thunderstorms that ever was known in these parts; and after he had made that prayer he forgot to pray again.[4] I expect there are many such in the world. But to proceed: The poor little Indian boy, when the Sabbath came, had nowhere to go to worship God, and so, like all other little boys who are left alone in the world, would stroll about the lots and meditate upon past times and listen to the little songsters of the forest, which would chaunt the praise of God for me, while there was none to take me by the hand and lead me to the holy place or to the fountain of blessedness. Now, if my face had been white, it would have been a town talk. But as it was an Indian face, no matter whether it was dirty or poor or whether I had clothing or not. But the judge has gone to the great Judge above, who will do right. I would not live with him, and he sold me, as a farmer would sell his sheep for the slaughter, without any of my knowledge whatever, to Mr. Williams, of New London; and through hypocrisy alone they carried me along to my place of destination. I had now arrived at the age of about eleven years and a half, and now I found that I had a new home; and in fact, I was not so much displeased with it as some might suppose, for now I found myself in a comfortable situation—enough to eat and drink, and things comfortable to wear—whereas before I was quite destitute of many things. This improvement somewhat settled my mind, and I became more contented. But soon I found that all his household wished me to become their servant, from the cook to the clerk. This I did not stomach well; it was too much for one to bear, to call every man "master." I thought it beneath my dignity; of course, there

4. The contrast Apess is drawing is between rote and spontaneous prayers. For an evangelical, the only genuine prayer comes from the heart, not from memorization. The jab at the judge is sharp, for only once has he been known to utter a "real" prayer and that because he was so frightened by a thunderstorm as to give it out involuntarily.

was war in the wigwam—who should be master. But Mr. Williams settled with us all, and with me in particular, as he said he meant to make me a good boy, but at the same time told me that I must obey the heads of his family, and all this was perfectly right; and some good, I think, was accomplished. However, I never cried out like the poor African, "Massa, Massa—Mister, Mister," but called them by their regular names.

Things now went on smoothly for some time. The general and his family generally attended the Congregational church or society on the Sabbath, to hear the word of God dispensed; though neither he nor his family were religious, yet they used to be often there; and their example was good so far as it went; and so I had an opportunity to attend with them. My mind was much occupied about those who preach the Gospel, there being a difference between those who preach and those who read.[5] I could discover this; the preaching that I formerly attended was with divine power, which made the language of the speaker eloquent and sublime, and withal called the attention of those who heard it to seek the salvation of their souls; while that of the latter, being a selection of fine sentences, and read off in an elegant style, which only seemed to please the ear and lull the people to sleep. How much better, then, to study and trust in God than to study and trust to head and pen; for a curse is pronounced upon all such: "Cursed is he that putteth his trust in an arm of flesh." And what is the difference whether a preacher puts it in his own arm or the arm of his neighbor? Now, I have not said this because I am biased by any sectarian principle whatever; I should condemn it in one sect as much as in another. But what said our Lord? He said to his servants, "Go and preach the Gospel to every creature." Why did he not say, "Go, read my Gospel to every creature?" Therefore, no man who reads his sermon can be justified in so doing; for Jesus has said, "Now are ye my disciples, if ye do whatsoever I have commanded you." And if they who are the servants of God go astray, and do wrong continually, and place things where they ought not to be, no wonder the churches are all the time in commotion. But to proceed:

After I had attended the meeting a while, I had a desire to attend Methodist meeting, in the same neighborhood. This was altogether new to me; but it was interesting to attend them, and so much so that I desired to be a constant attendant of them. By these meetings I was led to look more into the plan of salvation, that it was free for all: "Whosoever would, let him come and take of the waters of life freely."

It was now that the Lord began to revive his work. The powers of darkness began to gather round, that the light of the Gospel might be shut out. Beelzebub was busy, both day and night, to prevent good. He employed

5. That is, between those who preach without a written text and those who read their sermons.

all that would work for him, from the pharisee to the educated scholar in the desk, even down to the peasant and drunkard that reeled around in gutters and mud puddles in the street. It was now that these people had to suffer much; they were openly called the scum and filth of the earth, deceivers, and, in a word, all the calumny that could be heaped upon them, by those who ought to have known better. It was said that it was a disgrace for any character of respectability to attend these meetings. But I can say this much about it; I believe it arose from sectarian bigots. Not that I could suppose that they (the Methodists) were free from it, but have as much as their neighbors; and it is the case with all sects, that they are more or less bigoted. And if they are, they need not join with the devil's crew, to do all the hurt they can to one another. This, to me, does not look much like religion.

But the work of God rolled on, like an overwhelming flood. Persecution seemed to cement the hearts of the brethren and sisters together, and their songs were sweet. Their prayers and exhortations were like arrows sticking in the heart of their King's enemy, while the preachers poured the thunders of the law upon them, as if God himself had spoken to them, as he did to the children of Israel from Mount Sinai, that they should fear and tremble at his word.

My heart now became much troubled, and I felt determined to seek the salvation of my soul, for their sayings did not affect me much (although they did not want me to attend their meetings), though I had neither respectability nor character to lose but was like the partridge upon the mountain, a mark for them all to shoot at, and hiss at, and quack at—which often put me in mind of the geese and crows.[6]

But, notwithstanding, this sectarian nonsense raged most bitterly, and I do suppose that they who could help it would not be willing for their dogs to go there to meeting, for fear of bringing disgrace upon themselves. I would to God that people were more consistent than what they are. Say, would you like to lose everything that was near and dear to you, merely because your skin is white? I had to do it, merely because I had a red one. Judge ye, if this is right; and if not, stop where you are, and cease to do evil and learn to do well. But again, as I had no character to lose, I became a constant attendant on these meetings, and although a sinner before God, yet I had no disposition to make sport of the people of God or his word. Why I mention this is because so many go on purpose to sport with one another and make derision of the people of God, and those, too, who call themselves gentlemen and ladies. Such, how-

6. The pronouns can confuse here. "Their sayings" are those of the "respectable," like the Williamses who scorned the Methodists as vulgar and disreputable, while "their meetings" are those of the Methodists who welcomed the boy.

ever, disgrace themselves and are, in the judgment of good men, and their Maker, below the beasts of the field. Shame! shame! shame! to be so indecent, who boast of so much correctness and purity! But, notwithstanding the people would be so bad, yet the "Lord had respect unto his people, and his ears were open to the cries of his servants, and his ears were open to their supplication"; and in answer to prayer, he was pleased to revive his work; the Holy Ghost moved upon the face of the congregation; and his children were built up, and gathered strength at every meeting, and were built up in the most holy faith of the Gospel, and soon the power of the Holy Ghost fell powerfully among the people, so that the cries of the wounded were distinctly heard at every part of the house. The great Physician of souls was present, to heal all that would come to him and seek his favor. Thus the work of God went on most powerfully, so much so that Satan and his army retreated, at times, before it; and then would gather around it like a thick cloud of darkness, and mimic the catamount, or owls of the forest, or the young lion, which had lost its mother, and roaring to be answered. But the Lord assisted his servants to overcome them, through the word of his testimony.

It was now that conviction settled upon my mind, more and more; and I was more serious than usual. But being young, only about fourteen years of age, was somewhat flighty; though when I considered how great a sinner I was before God, and how often I had grieved the good Spirit of the Lord, my distress for mercy was very great.

At one of these meetings I was induced to laugh, not because I wanted to but to hide my distress from those around me. Being among the young people, I did not wish for them to know it; but such was my seriousness that it could not be hid, and I became affected, even unto tears, until they coursed down my cheeks like rain. And when the bold persecutors saw it, they inquired if I was one of the Lamb's people.

Brother Hill was at this time preaching from these words: "Behold the Lamb of God, who taketh away the sins of the world." He spoke feelingly of his (Christ's) sufferings on the cross; of his precious blood, that flowed like a purifying river from his side; of his sustaining the accumulated weight of the sins of the whole world; and dying to satisfy the demands of justice, which could only be appeased by an infinite atonement. I felt convinced that Christ had died for all mankind; that age, sect, color, country, or situation made no difference. I felt assured that I was included in the plan of redemption, with all my brethren. No one can conceive with what joy I hailed this new doctrine, as it was called. It removed all my excuses, and I freely believed that all I had to do was to look in faith upon the Lamb of God, who made himself a free-will offering for unregenerated and wicked souls, upon the cross. My spirits were depressed; my crimes were arrayed before me; and no tongue can tell the anguish of soul I felt. After meeting, I returned home with a heavy heart, determined to seek the salvation of my soul.

This night I slept but little; at times I would be melted down into tenderness and tears; and then again, my heart would seem as hard as adamant. I was awfully tempted; the evil one would try to persuade me that I was not in the pale of mercy. I fancied that evil spirits stood around my bed; my condition was deplorable, and awful; and I longed for day to break, as much as the tempest-tossed mariner, who expected every moment to be washed from the wreck he fondly clings to; so it was with me, upon the wreck of the world, buffeted by Satan, assailed by the world; sometimes in despair; then believing against hope; my heart, at times, seemed almost broke, while the tears of contrition coursed down my cheeks like rain.

But sin was the cause of all this, and no wonder; I groaned and wept; I had often sinned, and my accumulated transgressions had piled themselves as a rocky mountain upon my heart; and how could I endure it? The weight thereof seemed to crush me down; in the night seasons, I had fearful visions, and would often start from my sleep and gaze around the room, as I was ever in dread of seeing the evil one ready to carry me off. I continued in this frame of mind for more than seven weeks. My distress, finally, became so acute that the family took notice of it; some of them persecuted me because I was serious and fond of attending meetings. Now persecution raged on every hand, within and without; and I had none to take me by the hand and say, "Go with us and we will do you good." But in the midst of difficulties, so great to one only little more than fourteen years of age, I ceased not to pray for the salvation of my soul: Very often my exercises were so great that sleep departed from me. I was fearful that I should wake up in hell. And one night I was in bed mourning, like the dove for her absent mate, I fell into a doze. I thought I saw the world on fire; it resembled a large bed of coals, red, and glowing with heat; I shall never forget the impression it made upon my mind. No tongue can tell or possibly describe the agony of my soul; for now I was greatly in fear of dropping into hell, that awful place, where the smoke of their torments ascendeth up forever and ever. I cried earnestly for mercy; then I was carried to another place where perfect happiness seemed to pervade every part, and the inhabitants thereof. Oh, how I longed to be among them and partake of their happiness. I sighed to be freed from pain and misery; I knew that nothing but the attenuated thread of life kept me from sinking into the awful lake which I beheld. I cannot think it is in the power of human language to describe the feelings that rushed upon my mind at that moment, or thrilled through my veins; everything seemed to bear the signet of reality. When I awoke, I was glad to find it was a vision and not a reality. I went on from day to day, with my head bowed down, seeking the Savior of sinners, but without success. The heavens appeared to be brass; my prayers wanted the wings of faith to waft them to the skies. The disease of my heart increased; the heavenly Physician had not stretched forth his hand and poured upon my soul the panacea of the Gospel; the scales had not fallen from my eyes; and no ray of celestial light had dispelled the darkness that had gathered around my soul; the cheering sound of sincere friendship fell not upon my ear. It seemed as if I was friendless, unpitied, and unknown; and at times I wished to become a dweller in the wilderness. Who can wonder, then, that I was almost in despair, surrounded by difficulties and apparent dangers? But I was resolved to seek the salvation of my soul with all my heart; to trust entirely to the Lord and, if I failed, to perish pleading for mercy at the foot of the throne. I now hung all my hopes upon the Redeemer, and clung with indescribable tenacity to the cross, on which he purchased salvation for my soul, "the vilest of the vile." The result was such as is always to be expected, when a lost and ruined sinner throws himself entirely on the Lord—*perfect freedom.* On the 15th day of *March,* in the year of our Lord, 1813, I heard a voice saying unto me, in soft and soothing accents, "*Arise, thy sins that are many are all forgiven thee; go in peace and sin no more.*" There was nothing very singular, save that the Lord stooped to lift me up, in my conversion.

I had been sent into the garden to work, and while there, I lifted up my heart to God, when, all at once, my burden and fears left me; my soul was filled with love; love to God, and love to all mankind. Oh, how my poor heart swelled with joy! And I would cry, "Glory to God in the highest." There was not only a change in my heart but everything around me. The scene was entirely changed; the works of God praised him, and I saw in everything that he had made his glory shine. My love now embraced the whole human family; the children of God, I loved most dearly. Oh, how I longed to be with them; and when any of them passed me, I would gaze at them until they were lost in the distance. I could have pressed them to my bosom, as they were more precious to me than gold, and I was always loath to part with them whenever we met together. The change, too, was visible in my very countenance. I enjoyed great peace of mind, and that peace was like a river, full, deep, and wide, and flowing continually. My mind was employed in contemplating the works of God and in praising his holy name. I dwelt so particularly upon his mercy and goodness that I could praise him aloud, even in my sleep, and when I awoke, it was glory to God and the Lamb, and my heart burnt continually with the love of God. Well might the poet say,

> O for such love, let rocks and hills
> Their lasting silence break;
> And all harmonious human tongues
> The Savior's praises speak.

I continued in this happy frame of mind for some time; it was very pleasant to live in the enjoyment of pure and undefiled religion, and naught could I see but seas of rest and waves of glory before me. I wanted only the wings of angels to waft me to Paradise, that I might dwell around the throne of God forever. But alas! I dwelt in a tent below, that held me fast and would not let me go, and here to resist the fiend, the Christian's foe—to war, and tug, and toil at the oar of prayer, till time with me no more should be; and then, if faithful to my Lord, with all the faithful saints should be.

But here I can say, I had none to make me the object of their care, to encourage me to press forward in the ways of well doing. But, on the other hand, persecution raged most bitterly, and soon I was deprived of that privilege that was near and dear to me: such as the privilege of class meetings, and other means of grace, that are usually among the Methodists; and being young, I was again led astray. How hard it is to be robbed of all our earthly rights and deprived of the means of grace, merely because the skin is of a different color; such had been the case with me.[7] I would ask the white man if he thinks that he can be justified in making just such a being as I am, or any other person in the world, unhappy; and although the white man finds so much fault because God has made us thus, yet if I have any vanity about it, I choose to remain as I am, and praise my Maker while I live that an Indian he has made.

But again: The burden that was heaped upon me, at this time, was more than I could bear, being only about fifteen years old, and I now began to relapse back again into my former state. I now became acquainted with wicked and silly youths, and one of them whose name was *Miner* and myself agreed to try some other parts of the world. Children as we were, we made the best arrangements for our journey that we could; and so off we started and steered our course for New York. With difficulties and fears, we arrived there. Many of the people thought that we were sailor boys, as we informed them that we had been privateering and had been taken and set on a shore near New London and were going home to New York, to our parents; and it being wartime, we informed the people all we knew about it. When we had arrived at New York City, and almost alone in the world, and but little economy to take care of ourselves, we thought best to engage in the war.[8] So I became a musician in the army, while my comrade went on board of a privateer.

We now parted, and I went with the soldiers to Canada, where I experi-

7. In the 1837 edition this is revised to "with us poor colored people." At the end of this paragraph a similar revision implicates his experience with that of all people of color: "that Indians he has made."

8. The War of 1812. Apess enlisted in April 1813 when he was fifteen.

enced all the horrors of war; fought in the great Battle of Lake Champlain, with General McComb, with Hampton and Wilkinson, at the Mills. After the war was over, I went to Montreal and from thence to upper Canada, Fort Niagara; from thence to Kingston, and through the wilderness, and saw many of my brethren, who ornamented the wood with their camps and chanted the wild beasts of prey with their songs.[9] Being now satisfied with these regions and their curiosities, I now began to think of home and those kindred friends who had long before buried me beneath the sods of the forest, to behold my face no more forever here, being gone so long, nearly five years.

This journey was not instructing to the paths of virtue but of vice— though I did not forget the past, and often recollected those happy moments, and sighed on account of my condition, but had no heart to pray, no pious parents to instruct me, no minister of God's holy word to notice me and pour into my ear the blessed truths of God, but a poor, destitute, helpless child of the forest, all alone in the world, as it were. I now made the best of my way home to my kindred in the flesh, and when I arrived there, I found them surprised and rejoiced to see me on this side of the grave. After a while I became more steady and began once more to attend the worship of God, and had a desire to return from my backsliding state to the worship of God, that I might enjoy his smiles again. For it was now that I had become wretched and miserable through the deceitfulness of sin, and bad examples of the white soldiers, and nothing but thick darkness gathered around me; and, apparently, my situation was worse than before. It was now harder to seek the Lord than it was when I was young, for now my sins were redoubled; and it appeared indeed that there was no mercy for me. And when I went to pray and call upon God for mercy, I was met by the enemy of souls, who very readily thrusted a dart at me filled with a message of despair, that there was nothing but eternal death for me; that I had committed the unpardonable sin, by having sinned against the Holy Ghost, and it was all in vain for me to try again for help in God; that he was sure that I should make up his host in hell.[10]

My distress became more acute than ever; but I attended the meetings where God's children meet and at last I made known my distress to them; and they, the dear children of God, comforted me, by saying that Christ would have mercy upon the worst of sinners, and encouraged me to pray; and then prayed with and for me.

9. Apess was around the Bay of Quinte in Ontario, with either a community of Mohawks on the northeast shore or a community of Mississaugas on the southwest shore.

10. The unpardonable sin was despair, that is, to believe that one's own sin and sinfulness were greater than God's love and power.

I sought the Lord for weeks and months, and at last I began to see that I had received some of his divine approbation: To say that I immediately had as clear an evidence as I had before, I cannot. But when I acknowledged myself a sinner before the people and confessed what a sinner I had been, then the light of God's countenance broke into my soul, and I felt as if I were on the wings of angels and ready to leave this world. I united with the Methodists, and was baptized by immersion, and strove to walk with them in the way to heaven, and can say that I spent many happy hours with them in the worship of God; and to this day, I most heartily rejoice that I was brought again from the dead to praise God. After a while, I began to exercise my gift in the way of prayer and exhortation and was blest in so doing. I began to be exercised more abundantly about the salvation of precious souls and began to have a desire to call sinners to repentance in a public way; and it appeared I could not rest in any other way. But I knew that I was weak and ignorant as to the letter; and not only so, I was already a hissing-stock and a byword in the world, merely because I was a child of the forest; and to add any more occasion to the weak and scornful family of the whites was more than I wished to do; but there was no peace for me, either by day or night. Go I must, and expose my ignorance to the world, and strive to preach, or exhort sinners to repentance. I soon found men like adders, with poison under their tongues, hissing around me; and to this day, I find now and then one hissing at me. My trials again were many, and apparently more than I could bear; but I entreated of God to show me my duty and prayed to him for a token of his grace, when I went to call sinners to repentance. The Lord heard my prayer, and sent down his awakening power, and convinced sinners of the error of their ways; but I was too unbelieving, believing that I was not the character that God should take to thresh the mountains of sin. The angel of the Lord appeared to me in the visions of the night and read some extracts of John's Gospel. It appeared that before me there was a plain, and upon that the sun shone delightfully; but it was a difficult place for me to reach, being a dark and winding way, through mire, but I reached it; here I was encouraged by the angel to persevere. It was now, when I awoke, that I was troubled still the more; and night and day it was preach, preach, though many thought it would be a miracle for such an ignorant creature as I to preach the Gospel. But it is a fact that I had a difficult road to travel before I really got to preaching; but I can say that I have seen the salvation of the Lord in so doing, and God has made me, the unworthiest of all his servants, the humble, happy instrument in bringing many to bow at his scepter. To him be all the glory forever.

I would now say that I have been a regular member in the Methodist Episcopal and Protestant Methodist church for about nine years; in the Methodist Episcopal church I was an exhorter for eighteen months. I left them in good standing, and with good credentials on April 11, 1829, and united with the Protestant Methodists, not because I had anything very special against the former, any further than their government was not republican.[11] Their religion is as good as it ever was. I have been in the Protestant church something like four years, as a preacher of the Gospel; and in that time have received holy orders as an authorized minister of Christ, to attend to the duties of a pastor; and I am no sectarian whatever, but boldly declare that I have preached for all that would open their doors; and all sects have bid me welcome; and this is as it should be. May God pour his Spirit upon them all, and all the world. Amen.

William Apess

THE EXPERIENCE OF THE MISSIONARY'S CONSORT
(Written By Herself)

I was born in Lyme, Conn., A.D. 1788 on the third day of January. My father was a descendant of one of the Spanish islands, or a native of Spain. My mother was an English woman, a descendant of the Woods family of Lyme. My father died when I was small, and like all other fatherless children, I had to be placed out among strangers. My mother, having but little property and not being able to sustain me, being a poor child, this was done before I had arrived at my sixth year, and among people, too, who neither feared God nor regarded man but blasphemed their blessed Maker, and that too with the greatest impunity. The woman was a proud and haughty person and often raged most bitterly at me, and that too for the most trivial things. I had no pious parents or guardians to teach me the paths of virtue; I never recollect any serious impression made on my mind while I lived with these people, by their admonitions. One day it was suddenly suggested to my mind that God saw me, and I was afraid to die. I was guilty before him, and I wished to find some place to hide from his presence; but, since I have found Jesus precious to my soul, I have regretted that I sought him not when I was young; but I had none to lead me to the blessed fountain of holiness, where my sins might be washed away; there was none that cared for my precious soul.

I was now residing at Mr. D. Gillet's, in Lyme, being now about twelve years of age, and about this time a circumstance happened that it was thought best that I should go home. I went home and there stayed about two months, as senseless to the reality of a future state as the beasts of the field. And then I was again bound out to Mr. Aniel Ely, in Lyme, where I continued until I was

11. In 1837, "as I then understood it" is added, further softening any hint of his estrangement from the Methodist Episcopal church.

eighteen years of age. Mr. Ely was a member of the Presbyterian church. He used to say his prayers every Saturday night and Sunday morning; after a few times in attendance, I could say his prayer as well as he. I used to be at church on the Sabbath, but Mr. Ely never told me I had a soul to save or to lose. I could not tell what I went to meeting for, unless it was to see and be seen, and learn fashions; what the minister said, I understood not, nor did it affect my mind. Thus, I went on, careless and prayerless, for about two years. When I had advanced to fourteen years of age, there arrived in our neighborhood a missionary, by the name of Bushnell. Before I heard him preach, he paid us a visit, and hearing much about him, I was anxious to see him but did not wish for him to see me. I was afraid of ministers and professors of religion; I thought them a better people than others; but after tea, the missionary made his appearance to us in the room where the children were, and there he very affectionately exhorted us all. This was the first time that I had ever been warned to seek the salvation of my soul. His words sank deep on my mind; I began to weep as soon as he had left me; I went out, and for the first time I ever felt the need of praying or of a Savior; I knelt and poured out my soul to God, that he would have mercy upon me; although I had never seen anybody kneel, yet it was impressed on my mind that I must, and from that time I cried to God earnestly every day, during some months.

The missionary preached that Sabbath, and I attended all his meetings; the word was with power to my heart; I think he was the first man of God I ever heard preach. During his stay, he visited at our house several times and would always admonish me: I was pleased to hear him but dare not make known the exercises of my mind to him. Mr. Bushnell expressed himself in such a way that it had a powerful effect and made a lasting impression on my mind; that was, when he saw me employed about my daily work here, he hoped that he should meet me in heaven. I felt myself such a vile wretch, I could not see why he should speak so to me, a poor sinner. But I was ignorant of the power of divine grace, that could fit me for that place. While Mr. B. stayed, my impressions were deeper and deeper, and I was daily resolved to seek the Lord and leave the vanities of the world behind me. But he soon left the place, and when he was gone, there was not one in the place that ever afterward presented the subject to me, only in the way of derision; even the children would laugh at me and say that Mr. B converted me. I had plenty of such aid from old and young.

Mr. Ely, although a member of the church, never mentioned the subject of religion to me while I lived with him. I pray God to have mercy upon all such church members. But through all the opposition and persecution I had, I strove to seek the salvation of my soul and cry to God to help me; this I did for about six months, but I was tormented without and within. Mrs. Ely was a stepmother in the house and very wicked, and withal a very great tyrant: Sometimes she would get angry at the other children and beat me, and for the most trifling thing. She would say to me at times, when I was meditating upon death and judgment, that my head was full of the evil one, and so much so that I could not attend to what she wanted me to. But this only grieved me, and I would sorrow and weep in secret places. Here I would remark how much little children have to undergo, who are fatherless and motherless in the world, and what was I but a child? How much I wanted a tender, and affectionate, and pious mother to take me by the hand and instruct me, or some pious friend. How much good it would have done to me; but I had none but a wicked and an unholy tyrant to discourage me. But I leave her, as she has long since gone to a just God who will do right. Poor woman, she died as she lived, a poor and impenitent sinner. About this time the Methodists came into the neighborhood and held meetings about a mile off: There was everything said about them but good. It was said that they had the devil among them, and I believed it and would as soon go to the house of ill fame as I would to their meetings. This prejudice only came, however, by the hearing of the ear, which made me as foolish as thousands of others have been on the same account.

However, I continued to pray, but I was alone and I had no one to communicate my feelings to but the Lord, and he, at times, gave me sweet peace of mind; but I did not know that it was religion. I had no pious father or godly pastor to look after me; nor mother in Israel to take me by the hand and drop an encouraging word of sympathy over me; nor friends—none of these blessings was I favored with, and I am sure that I did not want the world any more then than now. But having no pious instructor or Christian examples before me, the enemy of my soul became too powerful for me. I had a proud heart, a tempting devil, an alluring world to flatter and decoy me away, and to its force I yielded—cast off fear and restrained prayer. Oh, how horrible was my situation now, and I again slid into rude company, gave way to the pride of my heart, and my most besetting sins were music and dancing. And how thankful I am that I was never led away, as many poor females are, to disgrace themselves forever, and sometimes to swift destruction and to a miserable hell. I went on now in the way of folly, but not without conscience giving me a check at times, till I was 23 years of age. I would read my Bible; at times, I would be displeased with it, and the grand enemy of my soul would tempt me not to believe it, that it was a libel upon the world, and for a while I tried to believe it. But there was a passage that so forcibly struck my heart that I could not doubt its correctness; that is, "Except ye be converted and become as a little child, ye can in no wise enter the kingdom of heaven." The reason why I felt so indifferent, I suppose it originated from my being at Hartford, Conn., where I learned more evil than good; for I used to attend all the parties of recreation that came in my way; and in reading those sacred pages, they condemned my former proceedings, and my heart was not willing to submit to them. But I would remark further; while I lived in Hartford, although I used to frequent the ball chamber, yet when I returned home and meditated on death, judgment, and eternity, it would blast all my imaginary happiness, and my heart would sink in sorrow down, because I was such a sinner. And while here in the city of Hartford, I heard of the Methodists, but it was only in the way of derision. I heard of their camp meetings, that they had the most awful works that ever was known, or heard of; and I believed it—and took no pains to inform myself but lived on the credit of hearsay.

But although I was such a wicked sinner, I could not bear the thought of going to hell. Yet I went on in rebellion against God and did not seek for instruction; if I had, I do not doubt that I should have found it. Yet I felt sensible that without religion I must go to hell. But when I arrived to the age of twenty-one, I thought I would abandon all hopes of heaven, and if I went to hell, I should not go alone—that I should have plenty of company; so I though I would rest easy where I was; and if I should live to old age, then I would seek the Lord and get ready to die. But how little did I think of the uncertainty of life. But being now at my mother's home, and having been informed that the Methodist meetings were about two miles off, and was strongly invited by one of my neighbors to go to meeting with her. So, notwithstanding I had united to make derision of them with the rest of the wicked, yet for the first time I thought that I would go, though all the neighbors around, with the exception of a few, told the same sad tale. Yet, thought I, it is no harm for me to go and hear for myself—so I went. I think I never shall forget the preacher's text; it was in Acts 24:25, "And as he reasoned of righteousness, temperance," etc. And as the words fell from the preacher's lips, so it seemed to sink with weight into my heart—and its powerful effect was very great. I was convinced that I was a sinner and must be lost without a Savior. I saw that I was to blame for the sins I committed, and no one else. I began to tremble like a Felix. I saw it would not do to put off repentance until old age, for I saw that time was short, and eternity near, and life uncertain, and death certain.

I ever afterward attended the poor, despised Methodist meetings; and while sitting under the preaching of the Gospel, I felt myself such a lost sinner that at times I could not but just refrain from crying aloud for mercy. But I grieved the Holy Spirit again and again. I was afraid of persecution—not being willing to give up my good name and become a follower of the meek and humble Jesus. Though conviction for sin did so powerfully sit upon me at times, I knew not what to do; yet, when my young mates came where I was, or

I with them, I would join with them in their folly. Oh, how hard it was to give them up, and the vanities of this life, for an interest in Christ Jesus. It is a wonder of mercy that he did not give me up to hardness of heart and to a reprobate mind.

I wanted religion in my own way, and had a wish to have it and keep it to myself. I kept along in this way about a year. I recollect at a thanksgiving, while at home, my mother wished me to attend with her on an evening visit to a neighbor's house; but I felt very indifferent about going; but to please her I gave my consent. But before we got to the house, I heard music and dancing: I wished to return and go no farther, for I knew that I had promised the Lord that I would not dance any more. I told my mother I did not wish to join them—but she insisted on my going, saying that "I was not obliged to dance"; so I yielded and went along; and when we arrived there, I was very soon asked to dance, but I refused, with a determination not to. But my mother said that, if she was as young as Mary, she would. Hearing her say so, I thought, if she would if she was able, surely it would be no hurt for me—so I went onto the floor, but not willingly; and when I began to dance, it seemed as if the floor would sink. I felt awfully—a condemned sinner before God. However, I stayed and spent the evening with them. I mention this to show how much parents may do in keeping their children from the kingdom of God: But my mother was irreligious, and I regret to this day that I had no pious parents or teachers to instruct me. But, after all, it is a wonder that God did not take me out of the world and send me to hell.

After I had arrived at my twenty-fourth year, the Lord seemed to blast all my earthly joys and schemes by sickness and disappointments, but I could see the hand of God in this; but what could it be for I was not aware—but thought God was angry with me, and I did not know what he was going to do with me. Surely he led me in a way I knew not.

At that time I was away from home, nursing a sick woman. One night after I had retired, I was reading a hymn—"Come humble sinners, in whose breast"—and when I had come to this verse:

> I'll go to Jesus, though my sins
> Hath like a mountain rose;
> I know his courts, I'll enter in,
> Whatever may oppose.

I here viewed Jesus in the flesh, while upon earth, going about doing good, and his followers with him—and sinners falling at his feet, crying for mercy—and Jesus saying, "Son, daughter, go in peace and sin no more; for thy sins, which are many, are all forgiven thee." There was such a deep sense of my transgressions before me, that I had committed against a holy God, that

I could hardly contain myself. I thought, if he had been here, how gladly would I have fallen at his feet and implored forgiveness at his hand. I can truly say that I felt the need of mercy but did not know how to obtain it: There was no one near me that prayed, and what to do I did not know. A thousand thoughts rushed through me as in a moment of time, but I tried to raise my heart to God, which seemed to quiet me a little. I was afraid to go to sleep, but sometime in the night I fell into a doze, and when I awoke it was impressed powerfully on my mind that I must break off my sins and go in secret and pray—but how to I knew not, I had been such a sinner before God; but I tried to lift my heart to God and continued to do so a number of times during the day. I broke off from my outward sins and strove to do better, but did not reveal my mind to any. I went home, burdened with sin and guilt. I found no peace. There was a gloom spread over creation, and death seemed to be written on all, I said, and I wanted nothing but a preparation for it—for I had no desire for the things of this world—and sometimes I thought I took comfort in trying to pray and singing one of Dr. Watts's psalms—to hope, to love, to pray, is all that I require. The enemy of my soul told me that I was good enough, that I could pray and praise, and that was all God required of me.

I now went about to establish my own righteousness; I was a godly, formal saint; a pharisee within. I fear thousands build upon the same sandy foundation that I was then building upon. I praise God while I am writing, that he was jealous of his own glory and soon divested me of my rags of self-righteousness and opened my eyes and showed me whereabouts I was—that I was a guilty, wretched, helpless sinner before him, and he only kept me from sinking down to the abyss of woe. I now read my Bible; but it condemned me. I became angry at it, and with God, and wished to cast it from me, and I thought it hard for me to submit to his will or go to hell. I envied all the dumb beasts of the field, because they were innocent and had no souls. The very pains of hell got hold of me; and I thought, if hell were as bad as my conscience, it might well be called hell.

However, I went to meeting, and said nothing to anyone, nor they to me. It happened that I was at a house where one of the class was employed, a very pious man. I made known my mind to him, and he encouraged me to be faithful. I informed him that I wanted to attend class; he informed his leader, and I had an invitation to attend and was thankful for the privilege; and when they asked me the state of my mind, I told them the exercises and desires that I had; and they exhorted me to be faithful, to seek the Savior of sinners. But I was so hard and stubborn that I despaired of mercy at his hand. My mind was now led back to my former days, when the Spirit of the Lord strove with me— I saw I might have had religion then, but now there was no mercy for me—for I had sinned away my day of grace. The enemy said that God was unjust and would not forgive my sins, because I had sinned so long, and I must go to hell and had better put an end to my existence and know the worst of my case. Although I saw the justice of God in condemning me, yet I was not willing to be miserable forever. I felt dejected, and cast down, and forsaken, and I wept before·the Lord. I was burdened, on account of my sins; and when I walked out it seemed as if the earth would sink under me, and I should go down to darkness and sorrow to receive the punishment due that my crimes had merited—the worst person then living was better than I was. I went mourning from day to day without any light of the Son to cheer the dungeon of my soul; pride, unbelief, self-will, all combined to keep me from the Savior of sinners. I doubted his power to save me, such a vile sinner as I was. I attended the meetings, and class, and from that dear people I was encouraged to press forward and obtain my object, the salvation of my soul. But when I was alone, my mind was filled with temptations and doubts and fears. I felt like a sinner justly condemned before God; I thought that if I should feel this distress for years, and then if God should pardon me, it would be an act of great mercy. I read my Bible and prayed, but my distress increased daily; my appetite forsook me: I wished for no kind of food whatever. And at night I was sleepless, and I had striven to make myself better by the works of the law—but that increased my pain the more.

The verse of a hymn came to me—"I can but perish if I go; I am resolved to try—for if I stay away, I know I shall forever die." I resolved to seek Jesus while I lived and, if I perished, to perish at his feet. My distress rolled on; I could not work. I could find no religion in reading or praying. I took my Bible one afternoon, not knowing where I was going; and it was rainy, so I thought I would stay until I found mercy, if mercy could be found. The Lord led me, for I never had been there before—for it was a complete shelter from the rain that was then falling. It was among the rocks; I spent the afternoon in reading, meditation, and prayer—hoping, believing, and doubting. I stayed there until it began to grow dark. Before I left the place I found some relief. I had some faith that Jesus had died to redeem my soul and had risen again for my justification.

When I got home it was so dark that I could not see to read. So I took my Bible and a lamp, and the first chapter that I opened to was John 19:30: "When Jesus therefore had received the vinegar, he said, It is finished; and he bowed his head and gave up the ghost." These words were applied to my heart—it seemed as if Jesus spoke to me himself and said, "All this I suffered for you, that you might live with me in heaven." The plan of salvation was now opened to my view. The Son of God was revealed to me by faith, in all his offices, as prophet, priest, and king. With pleasing grief and mournful joy, my spirit now was filled; that I had such a life destroyed, yet live by him I killed. I

wept and grieved because Jesus had died to reveal so vile a wretch as I. My
load of sin and fear of hell were gone; and then I was forcibly struck with these
lines of the poet:

> Come mourning souls, dry up your tears,
> And banish all your guilty fears.

My burden of sin now left me; my tears were dried up. I felt a sweet peace in
my soul but did not think this a change of heart.

I retired to rest, and there was a great calm. I awoke in the morning, and
my soul was drawn out after God; and when I arose and looked around me
upon the works of creation, everything wore a different aspect; everything I
saw praised God; and I felt as if I had long been shut up in prison—my bonds
were loosed, my chains were fallen off, and I was set at liberty. I wanted to
proclaim to the whole world what God had done for my soul, and to my
brethren and to my young mates, how happy I was and what a dear Savior I
had found. I thought that I would go publish it without delay; but I was
ignorant of the devices of Satan. He very readily informed me that if I did
nobody would believe me. I listened to him and went not. I have been sorry
ever since, that I was not obedient to the heavenly vision; I thought that, if a
soul had been once cleansed from sin, that doubts and fears and darkness
would never return to trouble that soul anymore—but in this I was mistaken,
for they soon returned. On Sabbath morning, May 1813, I went to meeting as
usual, but my mind was filled with darkness and unbelief. After preaching, we
had a class for the dear children of God to relate the exercises of their minds;
and while they were relating theirs, I felt encouraged to press forward, for
some of them spoke the feelings of my heart. But I did not tell them the
exercises of mine; and when they asked me, I told them I did not feel such a
burden, and felt determined to persevere.

They gave me their pious admonitions, and I praised God for such a
privilege to meet with his dear children. At the close of the meeting the
preacher prayed earnestly for me. The Lord heard and answered the prayer,
to the joy of my soul—for I felt peace with God through our Lord Jesus Christ
and wanted to praise him aloud; but again I grieved the Holy Spirit of God
and hid my talent in the earth, but they rejoiced and I kept silent—well might
it be said that the fear of man bringeth a snare. I felt a love for the dear people
of God and could join with them in worship but did not believe that God had
converted me into his grace. I returned home praising God but was afraid that
someone would hear me. I sung a verse of a hymn called the Good Shepherd:

> Come, good Lord, with courage arm us;
> Persecution rages here—

Nothing, Lord, we know can harm us,
While our Shepherd is so near.
Glory, glory be to Jesus,
At his name our hearts doth leap;
He both comforts us and frees us,
The good Shepherd feeds his sheep.

The last part of the verses spoke the sentiments of my heart. When I got home, I had a cross to take up, to confess to my mother. And the Lord gave me strength to do my duty; and after I had prayed with them, there was great peace that overspread my soul. I lived fearing and doubting until the next Thursday. And then I visited my brethren, where we had a prayer meeting— and then I strove to tell them what the Lord had done for my soul. So I lived along from one worship to another, and the old saints were instruments in the hands of God, in keeping me from falling a prey to the enemy of my soul and the alluring charms of this vain world.

The hearing of the old pilgrims' songs, and their sweet admonitions, attended to buoy me up and keep me from stumbling into the ditch of despair; for it stimulated me to move forward. And had it not been for them, I think I should have relapsed back again and sunk down into the cradle of carnal security—for it was a common saying, that after a soul was once converted, there was no more danger, although the word of God taught me different as well as his Spirit. But weak and feeble minds like mine are apt to be led astray. But I praise God for pious instructors, that pointed out the way and bade me persevere. Had they taught me different, no doubt I should have been like Mother Eve, who was so much deceived by the subtle foe—as you know that after God had told her not to eat the fruit of the garden which grew upon a certain tree, because it would be death. But Satan told her it would not be— but otherwise. And so he tells thousands; and it is to be feared that too many give way to his flattering charms and ruin their own souls.

But, friends, let them say what they will about the Methodists; I bless God that I ever knew them—for they taught me to believe in a present and full salvation, in order to obtain a crown of everlasting life. In June 1813, I joined the society,[12] and by this people, and the doctrines that they preached, I found it to be the power of God unto salvation to my poor soul. When I joined the Methodists, the preacher told me I must count the cost, that I must expect a great many falsehoods to be told about me. I found it even so. The wicked

12. This date appears as 1823 in the 1837 edition. I think the 1813 date is the probable one because Mary Woods seems to have fully converted by the time she and William Apess met—at a Methodist meeting.

soon began to accuse me of things that I had done which I never even had thought of. I tried by the aid of Heaven to keep a conscience void of offense before God and man; for I knew that I had peace with him. It is said that "He who will live godly in Christ Jesus shall suffer persecution." If they call the Master of the house Beelzebub, how much more will they of his household! So I resolved by the grace of God to persevere and give up all and take up the cross and follow Christ through evil report as well as good—for they that followed Jesus should not walk in darkness but have the light of life.

In July, myself and three other candidates were baptized by immersion by Elder Joel Winch, Salem, Conn. Truly the ordinance was blessed to me; it was a heaven below; a paradise, indeed, to my soul. I had such love, joy, and peace that I thought I never should doubt again—but in this I was mistaken; for it was not long before I doubted.

About August I went to camp meeting, hoping and praying that God would meet me there. I enjoyed myself well at the first of the meeting, but God had greater joy laid up for me. I tried in my weak way to exhort sinners and to be faithful to seek the salvation of their souls.

One day upon the campground, there was light from heaven shone into my soul, above the brightness of the sun. I lost sight of all earthly things— heaven was opened to my view, and the glory of the upper world beamed upon my soul. My body of clay was all that hindered my flying up to meet Jesus in the air. How long I remained in this happy frame of mind I do not know. But when I came to my recollection, my Christian friends were around me singing the sweet songs of heaven; and I thought I was in the suburbs of glory. And when I saw them, they looked like angels, for they were praising God. I felt the love of God like a river flowing into my soul. From that time until the close of the meeting, I was happy. I now returned home rejoicing in God my Savior. I thought that I never should be troubled with doubts and fears—but I was mistaken as before. The enemy of my soul tempted me, and I again gave way, and like Samson I lost all my strength, and I doubted of God's power to save me.

There was much said about sanctification, among our Methodist brethren—they said it was possible for God to cleanse us from all sin and urged the members of our church to seek it and not rest short of it—while others opposed it and said it was impossible to live without sin in this life and to be cleansed from all unrighteousness, boldly denying the power and efficacy of his blood. I was weak and unbelieving and finally doubted it myself, although I read it was the will of God, even our sanctification—and if we confess our sins, he is faithful and just to forgive us our sins, and the blood of Jesus cleanses us from all unrighteousness. I asked the Lord, in humble prayer, if this was attainable, and to show me what I am by nature, and what I ought to be by grace—for I was sure that I wanted as much grace as anybody in the world, to get through it.

I prayed daily for the Lord to enlighten me and teach me the way; for I wished to lay a sure foundation for the time to come. I continued my petition about one month; the Lord heard and answered my prayer and opened my eyes, and I saw if I was not fully saved from sin, and made holy, I could never enter into the kingdom of God, for God was holy, and heaven was a holy place, and without holiness no man should see the Lord.

I from that time read my Bible more diligently, and sought the Lord, by fasting and prayer, with a full determination not to stop, short of full redemption in the blood of Christ. I went to a quarterly meeting in Groton, Conn.; and there God manifested himself to me in such a powerful manner at that time that I fell prostrate upon the floor, insensible to all below; the last time I fell, I felt the blood of Jesus go through every avenue of the soul and body, cleansing me from the filthiness of the flesh and spirit. The Spirit bade me arise and tell what God had done for my soul; but I was again disobedient. After that, I was almost in despair, through unbelief. I struggled in darkness for some time; at last a divine ray of light broke into my soul. I then promised the Lord, if he would give me the evidence of full redemption in my heart, that I would proclaim it to all the world, come what would.

I attended a camp meeting, at Wilbraham, Mass. The power of the Lord was manifested in a wonderful manner, and there was a general cry among believers, for full redemption in the blood of Jesus; and I felt the cry in my own heart. I prayed, and cried, and struggled, and almost despaired of obtaining my object. But before the meeting closed, God in Christ showed himself mighty to save and strong to deliver. I felt the mighty power of God again, like electric fire, go through every part of me, cleansing me throughout soul, flesh, and spirit. I felt now that I was purified, sanctified, and justified. I had no fears. I could now shout victory through the blood of the Lamb. The words of the poet would best express my feelings:

> That sacred awe—that durst not move,
> All the silent heaven of love.

From that time until now, I have never doubted the power of God, to save all who by faith would come unto him; that is about seventeen years ago; and I find him still the same unchangeable, blessed Savior, his mercy always full and boundless as the ocean. I find it as good to my soul now as it was then; yea, I can say that it grows brighter and brighter, and do expect it will, even to the perfect day, if I am faithful. Then, through the merits of Jesus, I expect to hear the welcome sound, "Come, ye blessed of my Father, inherit the kingdom prepared for you from the foundation of the world," where all tears shall be wiped away from our eyes, and there with the happy throng shout and sing our sufferings over, around the throne of God. Then I should behold that great and innumerable company "that came out of great tribulation, and washed their robes, and made them clean and white in the blood of the Lamb," and have overcome, through the word of his testimony. There we shall be at rest, and the wicked shall cease from troubling us. Glory fills my soul while I meditate upon the moment when, through grace, I shall unite with them there.

I have now given you a sketch of the dealings of God with one of his most unworthy creatures. I am a spared monument of his mercy; and through his rich grace I hope to stand fast until he takes me from time to enter into his heavenly kingdom. May this be the happy lot of us all, is the prayer of your unworthy writer.

Mary Apess

The Experience of Hannah Caleb
(by the Missionary)

I was born in Groton, Conn. My mother died when I was about six years old. Her dying request was that I might be placed among educated people, who would teach me to read God's holy word. I accordingly was placed in a white family to be brought up. The gentleman's name, with whom I was placed, was Mr. James Avery, where I continued twelve years. They were a pious people, and by them I was instructed in the paths of virtue. But how much I have to regret that I did not take heed to my ways and, in the days of my youth, seek the salvation of my soul—then I should have been prepared to meet those troubles and trials which are incident to human life. But oh! how dark and dreary is the world without the sun! So is the way of sinners without the Sun of righteousness, to cheer and light up their dark and gloomy paths, through this wilderness world. But let us return: At the age of nineteen years I was married and had ultimately five children. My husband was a soldier in the French army and died in Canada, and with this trial I met with many more— the loss of all my dear children. And when the bosom friend, the darling of all my earthly career, was gone, with whom I should no more associate in time, it was almost too much for me to bear. But oh! when I turned to look for my children, at the seats and the table that they once surrounded, and at their pillows, which I had watched over with the affection of a fond mother, and had often pressed them to my breast, while tears fell like rain from their sparkling eyes upon my bosom, and had strove to hush them! But behold, they were no more, but all of them locked up in the cold caverns of the earth, and I their faces no more to behold in time—they were fled to the world of spirits, to him who had created them.

Thus my husband was gone—the darling of my heart—with my babes, the sweet objects of my care: Thus, being stripped of my earthly glory, I was left naked and wounded. I now became alarmed about my future welfare— for the Lord was at this time pleased to discover to me the lost condition of my poor soul. My conviction of sin was severe, but notwithstanding this, I was indifferent—not knowing how to help myself; but the anguish of my soul which I felt, no tongue can tell—for it was keen and pungent; and withal I felt a great enmity to the Christian religion, often wishing, in the depravity of my heart, I had been left like the rest of my kindred, ignorant and unknown. This may be surprising to some, but I can assure you there was a cause for this. I saw such a great inconsistency in their precepts and examples that I could not believe them. They openly professed to love one another, as Christians, and every people of all nations whom God hath made—and yet they would backbite each other, and quarrel with one another, and would not so much as eat and drink together, nor worship God together. And not only so, the poor Indians, the poor Indians, the people to whom I was wedded by the common ties of nature, were set at naught by those noble professors of grace, merely because we were Indians—and I had to bear a part with them, being of the same coin, when in fact, with the same abilities, with a white skin, I should have been looked upon with honor and respect.

But it is a fact that whites, with the same principle, would turn against their own kin, if the providence of God should have happened to change the shades of their complexion, although the same flesh and feelings. How must I feel, possessing the same powers of mind, with the same flesh and blood, and all we differed was merely in looks? Or how would you feel? Judge ye, though you never have been thrust out of society, and set at naught, and placed beyond the notice of all and hissed at as we have been—and I pray God you never may be. These pictures of distress and shame were enough to make me cry out, Oh horrid inconsistency—who would be a Christian? But I remark here that I did not understand frail nature as I ought, to judge rightly. And I would remark here that these feelings were more peculiar 70 years ago than now—what their feelings would be now, if the Indians owned as much land as they did then, I cannot say. I leave the man of avarice to judge.

But we observe further: The Lord was pleased in great mercy to continue the work of grace upon my heart, so I made bold to inquire by going from one Christian friend to another, asking questions about the way and what I must do to be saved. They said that I must pray, and look to the Lord as my Savior and friend. They told me that Jesus Christ died for sinners, even such as I, who was the chief of sinners. This encouraged me to pray, but I could find no comfort in so doing. I continued almost a year between hope and despair, wretched and miserable, without God and without hope in the world. The grand enemy of all good strove to decoy my mind away from my desired object and had well-nigh effected his scheme, for he suggested to me that there was no mercy for such sinners as I was. I used to roam whole days in my native forest, weeping and wailing on account of my sins, seeking the Savior of sinners—friendless, as I thought, unpitied and unknown. As I was walking by the side of a large pond, the enemy whispered to me to throw myself in and there end my days of sorrow and affliction. I was quick to obey. I got upon a log for that purpose; but a voice seemed to say to me, "Hannah, my mercy is as free for thee as this water, and boundless as the ocean." The tempter fled; my mind was calm, and I returned home, thinking that my distress would return no more; but in this I was disappointed. Soon all my doubts returned, and I could say with Job, "Thou hast shaken me to pieces; all my bones are out of joint." I was very weak, eating but just enough to keep soul and body united, often sleeping on the cold ground, and frequently not closing my eyes for nights together. However, I sometimes took great comfort in visiting the dear children of God, some of whom I went many miles to see, and hear them converse and pray for me. They pitied me and strove to comfort me, but all in vain.

I went out one evening, thinking that I should not return anymore, to behold my kindred in the flesh, or see the morning dawn; and there I prostrated myself before God and lifted up my hands to heaven, and, in the language of parting friends, I bade farewell to the moon, to the stars, and all creation, this earthly vision no more to behold in time. But withal I prayed that if it was God's will I might live a while longer—for I was not ready to die—and see those praying people, and hear one more prayer for my perishing soul, that I might be saved from hell and everlasting destruction, from the presence of God, and the glory of his power forever: For surely I thought it would be the place of my abode forever. But the Lord heard my prayer and spared me; and when the morning beamed forth, and my eyes caught her rising, I exclaimed, "Oh, that I might hear one more prayer for my poor soul." But it was suggested to me that Christians could not help me. I then turned from the world and the prayers of the saints and went into the wilderness and sat myself down, and I had an impression that I must sing. I thought, how could I sing of redeeming grace and dying love? Oh, the answer was, "Sing, for his mercy endureth forever." I must praise God for that; but where to begin I knew not, but thought I would try. So I began this way: "Glory to God the Father, glory to God the Son, glory to God the Holy Ghost, glory to God alone." After I had done singing, I had a desire to pray, but I thought, what shall I say? "Oh, I am a poor sinner. Lord have mercy upon me, a poor sinner." As I said so, glory seemed to break in upon my soul, and I was dissolved into the love of God, apparently, soul, body, and spirit. The heavens seemed to descend, and with them an innumerable company of angels, and the spirits of the just made perfect. They seemed to throng me; I was overcome with the vision. My whole soul was lost in wonder, love, and praise to God. I was enabled to join the heavenly company, and sing the wonders of redeeming grace and dying love.

My sins were all gone; I felt no longer their burden; I was transported, as it were, to the third heaven. This was about nine o'clock in the morning. Thus you see, my friends, that I was all night in prayer to God; and as I observed, the Lord pitied me and washed away all my sins. I then returned to my Christian friends with the lightness of an angel, with my heart tuned to sing the praise of God and the Lamb, with them, who had struggled so hard at the throne of grace for me. And I began to publish to them what the Lord had done for my soul, and warning sinners wherever I went to flee from the wrath to come.

Surely, I could say, "Old things are passed away, and behold, all things are become new." I could say there was no more enmity in my heart, that I loved white people as well as my own. I wonder if all white Christians love poor Indians. If they did, they would never hurt them anymore. And certainly, if they felt as I did, they would not. For I could say, as John said, "He that is born of God, has the witness in himself."

Thus I went on from day to day, in the service of my God, praising him all the while, and no cloud to darken my day. Oh, how happy, happy, was my soul, continually full of glory, glory.

Here the publisher would take the liberty of making a few remarks. Not being personally acquainted with Sister Caleb, I am not able to give her age and date of her conversion, precisely. But, being furnished by a young lady of respectability and piety with a copy, I have, therefore, no doubt of its authenticity. But nearly all my relations and a part of my family were acquainted with her personally. And here I would say a few things which you may place confidence in, respecting her. This dear child of the forest was translated into the kingdom of God, as near as we can learn, at the age of forty years; and as far as we can learn, she lived faithful through life. Sister Caleb was remarkable for her liberality, so that she not only had the precept but the example. She knew no sect but that of the Nazarenes; for she would go into all houses of worship and exhort sinners, and eat and drink at the Lord's table wherever it was spread, to show forth his death till he come; though she herself united to the Free-Will Baptists, to be under their watchful care.

Sister Caleb was also noted by all sects to be an example of piety; to all the world she was useful in temporal matters, such as teaching the young children of her tribe to read, while at other times she would instruct them and others, by precept and example, in the way to heaven and happiness. I can tell you, friends, that she lived in the faith of the Gospel; and thus lived and died our good sister, in the Lord, after nearly half a century from her conversion. She fell asleep in the arms of Jesus and went down to the grave with a joyful hope, big with immortality, of a glorious resurrection in Christ at the last trump, while her soul was wafted upon the wings of angels to the spirit land, to dwell around the throne of God forever and ever. There her trials are at an end; there she dwells in seas of rest, while before her, waves of glory roll, and shouts of glory echo from the throne.

W.A.

The Experience of Sally George
(by the Missionary)

I was born in Groton, Conn., 1779, and was brought up without any education, as to understanding the letter in any way whatever. And although there were many around us who were very zealous that we should have instruction, and be brought up well, yet but little was done toward it, I being left in general to wander to and fro, up and down the forest with my native kin. But surely I have many things to praise God for. Although I had not those inestimable privileges that some had and do have, yet I can say that I had some that many do not have, in time; there are many of my brethren who do not that are in the wide and western world. For they do not enjoy any instruction whatever. While poor me, although ignorant and unknown, yet I had some precious privileges: such as hearing God's holy word, and having good advice from those who were mothers in Israel. And, taught by the Spirit, they would beseech of me to be reconciled to God, and they were those of my own kin; and often they would do it with streaming eyes and melted hearts. Sometimes I would take a degree of interest in it, and at other times I would be quite indifferent about it; and at other times my young mates would lead me astray with their rudeness, being only about twelve or thirteen years old.

I continued in this way for some time, between hope and despair; but they continued to call after me, and the Holy Spirit seconded their efforts constantly, and often it was so powerful that my little heart would melt down into tenderness, and what to do with myself I knew not. I felt at times melancholy and dejected; but, notwithstanding this, I was encouraged by many to seek the salvation of my soul. But it was hard to leave my young mates; yet without religion I knew that I must be miserable and wretched forever. But what to do I did not know, and how to pray I knew not. I wandered up and down in the forest, weeping and mourning on the account of my sins, not knowing that I ever should enjoy happiness either in time or eternity. The enemy now would take the advantage of my youthful mind and suggest to me that there was no happiness for me, I must spend all the rest of my days in sorrow. The enemy of my soul followed hard after me and withal tempted me to destroy myself.

I had become now a wanderer alone, as it were, in my native woods; and one day as I was passing by a large, deep brook, the enemy of my soul tempted me to destroy myself in that place, by casting myself in. But I strove to raise my little heart to God, that he would have mercy upon my soul and save me. While thus exercised in prayer to God, for his kind protection, I fell to the earth as one dead, under the power of God. And while in this situation, I saw the pit of destruction opened for poor sinners; it was no imagination either, it was a solemn reality, it was plain before me. My soul was in sore distress, and I expected nothing but hell for my portion forever. I lay in this situation for some time as helpless as an infant, begging for the mercy of God, promising to him that I would be faithful to serve him all the days of my life. The Lord heard my prayer and sent down his melting grace into my soul; and before I arose from the ground I was translated into the kingdom of God's dear Son; for when I came to myself, I was praising God; there was a change in everything around me, the glory of the Lord shone around, all creation praised God, my burden and my fears were gone, the tempter had fled, and I was clothed, and in my right mind, sitting at the feet of Jesus.

I now returned home to my friends, and began to exhort my young mates to repentance, and to tell all that came in my way what the Lord had done for my soul. I then went to the church and told it there, and the dear children of God received me. I then with a servant of God went down to the banks of the river and was buried with Christ by immersion beneath the great water; and when I came up out of the water the glory of God descended and lighted upon my soul; and so I could rejoice continually, and say the one half was never told me about this Jesus whom many deride. "*Behold ye despisers, wonder and perish; I work a work in your day ye shall in no wise believe, though a man declare it unto you.*" And although I could not read, the Spirit of the Lord was with me to instruct me in the way of holiness, and upon my heart was printed the image of my Savior, by the washing of regeneration and renewing of the Holy Ghost. My soul was bathed in the love of God, it was glory, and I was lost in wonder, love, and praise. I forgot all things here below and rode in the chariot of his love daily. Bless the Lord, O my soul, and all my powers, soul and body, praise him, for glory is his due forever and ever. Amen—so let it be.

* * *

I would remark here that this female was an aunt on my father's side, and we had a personal acquaintance with each other. She belonged to the same church that Sister Caleb did, and they were well acquainted with each other. She was a member of the church about thirty years, and for the most of the time, as far as I can learn, she lived in the life and power of religion. I have attended a great many meetings with Sister George, and I do not recollect that she ever had a barren season to her soul. She often meted out to my soul the sincere milk of the word, which gave me strength in the Lord to persevere. The Lord, of a truth, was with her. She was always diligent to seek Jesus in the way. The fences, the groves, the forest—all will witness to the fact.

Her organic power of communication, when tuned with heavenly zeal and burnt with heavenly love, was delightful, charming, and eloquent. I never knew her to speak unless the congregation was watered by an overwhelming flood of tears. She feared not to warn sinners to repentance while she lived. She was no sectarian; she would go among all orders of Christians and worship God with them, and was entirely free so to do. And I believe that she felt as much for her white neighbors as for her own kindred in the flesh.

She was counted almost a preacher; her language was free, lively, and animating. She was also very industrious and active; her limbs would play as lively over the ground as a deer. I have set out to walk with her twenty miles to a meeting, several times in my life, and generally, I had to keep upon the slow pace to keep up with her. In three hours and a half from the time we started, we were there. She was also skilled in doctoring the sick, and was useful wherever she went; and in this way procured for herself a very great share of Christian and friendly patronage among all who knew her. And while visiting the sick she would often pour into their ear the balm of consolation and refer them to the blessed Jesus, who could heal both soul and body. Where she met with the sin-sick soul, she would pour into their ears the oil of joy and point them to Jesus, who taketh away the sin of the world, the only sovereign remedy for sin-sick sinners. Our sister was noted generally by all for her piety through life.

At the close of her life, there was a remarkable circumstance which took place, that is, respecting a visit which she desired to make to a neighboring village about eight miles off. But I would remark that previous to this she was much debilitated in body, which was caused by a lingering disease, supposed to be somewhat dropsical and consumptive, and did not at times keep about but was confined to her bed. She lived a widow, and withal very comfortable, and used to entertain all her brethren that came to her. There were some of her brethren whom she desired to see, and said the Lord would give her strength to perform the journey; and so she arose, as it were, from a sickbed, and through the strength of the Lord she was enabled to go; and while there, she enjoyed some Christian conversation, had a few good meetings, and bade her brethren farewell, to meet no more in time; and returned home to die. She was now composed, and ready to die—and in two weeks afterward, she fell asleep in the arms of Jesus, without a struggle or a groan, May 6, 1824, aged forty-five years.

At the last, the fear of death was taken away, and her dying bed was glorious and interesting. Her friends were many, both natives and whites. The whites paid to her remains the last tribute of respect, which is due to Christians, and united in shedding the tears of sympathy and depositing her remains in the dark and lonesome caverns of the earth, there to remain, locked up in the cold and icy arms of death—till the blast of the Archangel shall blow out the sun and pour the stars upon the earth like rain; then shall her ransomed dust revive, and in the Savior's image rise. But while she sleeps in dust below, she bathes her weary soul in seas of heavenly rest, and not a wave of trouble rolls across her peaceful breast—Oh reader, strive to meet her there.

W.A.

The Experience of Anne Wampy
(by the Missionary)

In the year 1831, I was sent by the New York annual conference of the Protestant Methodists to visit this tribe and preach to them. Being my native tribe, I took pleasure in so doing; and when I arrived to the place of my destination, I found them a poor, miserable company. But I intend to speak further in another place and shall proceed with her experience.[13]

I commenced exhorting them to flee the wrath to come—there was an old veteran of the woods, who despised all that was said to her upon the subject of salvation and would use very bad language in her way, being not able to speak plain English. However, the Lord reached her heart, and many others, and there was a work of God among us. Sister Anne was brought to bow and humble herself at the feet of Jesus, after she had experienced the holy religion of Jesus. She then was free to tell the exercises of her mind, and not till then. We will give it to you in her own language; it is broken, but you can understand it. She began thus:

13. In the 1837 edition Apess revises this to begin: "In the year 1831, I visited the Pequot Indians, a small remnant left from the massacre of the whites, who are now lingering in a miserable condition upon the banks of the River Thames, apparently unpitied and unknown. But being an Indian, and somewhat connected with the tribe, I took pleasure in offering to them the word of life, and to warn them to flee from the wrath to come. It cannot be wondered at, that it excited attention among old and young."

When Christians come to talk with me, me no like 'em; me no want to see 'em; me love nobody; I want no religion. But Sister Amy no let me alone; she talk a great deal to me about Jesus. Sister Apess, too, come talk pray for me. I be afraid I should see 'em, and me no want to hear 'em; by me, by me come trouble very much, me very much troubled. Me no like Christians, me hate 'em, hate everybody. By me, by me very much troubled; me get sick, me afraid I die; me go pray, go off all alone in the woods; me afraid I go to hell, me pray. By me, by Jesus, come take me by the hand, lead me a great way off, show me one place look like hell; me come close to it so me feel it, me afraid I fall in, me cry to Jesus to have mercy on poor me. He take me by the hand again and lead me back, show me one great mountain all full of crevices; he say I must make that all smooth before I come again. I say hard work; I afraid I go to hell at last. I pray I look to Jesus. By me, by me give up; then me feel light, like one feather; me want to die, me want to fly—me want to go home; me love everybody, me want to drink no more *rum*. I want this good religion all the time.

She now began to exhort sinners. "I wish I could talk like white folks, me would tell everybody how I love Jesus." Then she said to the young people, "Don't do like I done, me old sinner, great many years me sin, do wickedly. Come, love Jesus; I want everybody to come love Jesus. Oh, how I love Jesus; me want everybody to pray for me, so I get to heaven where Jesus is." She looked upon me, just as I was about to leave her, and with streaming eyes said, "Pray for me that I go to heaven." And while I was thus beholding her face, and viewing the tears streaming down her furrowed cheeks, it did me good, for I beheld glory beaming in her countenance, which bespoke the expression of the inward man.

Our sister was born in Groton, Conn., A.D. 1760; lived in sin rising 70 years, brought up in ignorance and prodigality till old age, and then snatched as a brand from the burning, and translated into the glorious light of the Gospel, and made an heir of all things. How good and kind is God to all men; notwithstanding they live long in sin, and rebel against him, yet he is willing to have mercy upon all that will come unto him, let them be ever so great and unprofitable sinners.

Should this happen to fall into the hands of any old transgressor, that has not become wise above what is written, I hope they will remember that they will want Master Jesus as well as Sister Anne Wampy.[14] Lord help, Amen.[15]

William Apess

14. Apess added the following here in the 1837 edition: "Though many, no doubt, will even ridicule the idea of doing as this poor pagan, but in order for any sinner, rich or poor, to enter the

kingdom of heaven, they must be first purified in order to enter into so pure a place as heaven; and this is reasonable doctrine. Depend upon it, sinners, it was the intent of Christ's sufferings; and the end of his sufferings can be answered in no other way than upon the conditions of your repentance, and a reform of your wicked ways."

15. Anne Wampy was memorable to more than one person. The Reverend John Avery recalled her years later in his fine local history, *History of the Town of Ledyard, 1650–1900* (Norwich, CT: Noyes and Davis, 1901), 259–60: "I remember, when I was quite a small boy, one Ann[e] Wampy used to make an annual trip in the early spring past my home up through Preston City, Griswold and Jewett City, selling the baskets she had made the previous winter. When she started from her home she carried upon her shoulders a bundle of baskets so large as almost to hide her from view. In the bundle would be baskets varying in size from a half-pint up to five or six quarts, some made of very fine splints, some of coarse, and many skillfully ornamented in various colors. Her baskets were so good that she would find customers at almost every house. And after traveling a dozen or twenty miles and spending two or three days in doing it her load would be all gone. Then she would start on her homeward journey, and, sad to relate, before she had reached her home a large part of what she had received for her baskets would have been expended on strong drink."

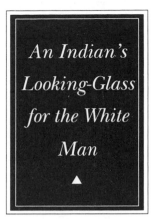

An Indian's Looking-Glass for the White Man

▲

Having a desire to place a few things before my fellow creatures who are traveling with me to the grave, and to that God who is the maker and preserver both of the white man and the Indian, whose abilities are the same and who are to be judged by one God, who will show no favor to outward appearances but will judge righteousness. Now I ask if degradation has not been heaped long enough upon the Indians? And if so, can there not be a compromise? Is it right to hold and promote prejudices? If not, why not put them all away? I mean here, among those who are civilized. It may be that many are ignorant of the situation of many of my brethren within the limits of New England. Let me for a few moments turn your attention to the reservations in the different states of New England, and, with but few exceptions, we shall find them as follows: the most mean, abject, miserable race of beings in the world—a complete place of prodigality and prostitution.

Let a gentleman and lady of integrity and respectability visit these places, and they would be surprised; as they wandered from one hut to the other they would view, with the females who are left alone, children half-starved and some almost as naked as they came into the world. And it is a fact that I have seen them as much so—while the females are left without protection, and are seduced by white men, and are finally left to be common prostitutes for them and to be destroyed by that burning, fiery curse, that has swept millions, both of red and white men, into the grave with sorrow and disgrace—rum. One reason why they are left so is because their most sensible and active men are absent at sea. Another reason is because they are made to believe they are minors and have not the abilities given them from God to take care of themselves, without it is to see to a few little articles, such as baskets and brooms. Their land is in common stock, and they have nothing to make them enterprising.

Another reason is because those men who are Agents, many of them are unfaithful and care not whether the Indians live or die; they are much imposed upon by their neighbors, who have no principle. They would think it no crime to go upon Indian lands and cut and carry off their most valuable timber, or anything else they chose; and I doubt not but they think it clear gain. Another reason is because they have no education to take care of themselves; if they had, I would risk them to take care of their own property.

Now I will ask if the Indians are not called the most ingenious people among us. And are they not said to be men of talents? And I would ask: Could there be a more efficient way to distress and murder them by inches than the way they have taken? And there is no people in the world but who may be destroyed in the same way. Now, if these people are what they are held up in our view to be, I would take the liberty to ask why they are not brought forward and pains taken to educate them, to give them all a common education, and those of the brightest and first-rate talents put forward and held up to office. Perhaps some unholy, unprincipled men would cry out, "The skin was not good enough"; but stop, friends—I am not talking about the skin but about principles. I would ask if there cannot be as good feelings and principles under a red skin as there can be under a white. And let me ask: Is it not on the account of a bad principle that we who are red children have had to suffer so much as we have? And let me ask: Did not this bad principle proceed from the whites or their forefathers? And I would ask: Is it worthwhile to nourish it any longer? If not, then let us have a change, although some men no doubt will spout their corrupt principles against it, that are in the halls of legislation and elsewhere. But I presume this kind of talk will seem surprising and horrible. I do not see why it should so long as they (the whites) say that they think as much of us as they do of themselves.

This I have heard repeatedly, from the most respectable gentlemen and ladies—and having heard so much precept, I should now wish to see the example. And I would ask who has a better right to look for these things than the naturalist himself—the candid man would say none.

I know that many say that they are willing, perhaps the majority of the people, that we should enjoy our rights and privileges as they do. If so, I would ask, Why are not we protected in our persons and property throughout the Union? Is it not because there reigns in the breast of many who are leaders a most unrighteous, unbecoming, and impure black principle, and as corrupt and unholy as it can be—while these very same unfeeling, self-esteemed characters pretend to take the skin as a pretext to keep us from our unalienable and lawful rights? I would ask you if you would like to be disfranchised from all your rights, merely because your skin is white, and for no other crime. I'll venture to say, these very characters who hold the skin to be such a barrier in the way would be the first to cry out, "Injustice! awful injustice!"

But, reader, I acknowledge that this is a confused world, and I am not seeking for office, but merely placing before you the black inconsistency that you place before me—which is ten times blacker than any skin that you will find in the universe. And now let me exhort you to do away that principle, as it appears ten times worse in the sight of God and candid men than skins of color—more disgraceful than all the skins that Jehovah ever made. If black or red skins or any other skin of color is disgraceful to God, it appears that he has disgraced himself a great deal—for he has made fifteen colored people to one white and placed them here upon this earth.

Now let me ask you, white man, if it is a disgrace for to eat, drink, and sleep with the image of God, or sit, or walk and talk with them. Or have you the folly to think that the white man, being one in fifteen or sixteen, are the only beloved images of God? Assemble all nations together in your imagination, and then let the whites be seated among them, and then let us look for the whites, and I doubt not it would be hard finding them; for to the rest of the nations, they are still but a handful. Now suppose these skins were put together, and each skin had its national crimes written upon it—which skin do you think would have the greatest? I will ask one question more. Can you charge the Indians with robbing a nation almost of their whole continent, and murdering their women and children, and then depriving the remainder of their lawful rights, that nature and God require them to have? And to cap the climax, rob another nation to till their grounds and welter out their days under the lash with hunger and fatigue under the scorching rays of a burning sun? I should look at all the skins, and I know that when I cast my eye upon that white skin, and if I saw those crimes written upon it, I should enter my protest against it immediately and cleave to that which is more honorable. And I can tell you that I am satisfied with the manner of my creation, fully— whether others are or not.

But we will strive to penetrate more fully into the conduct of those who profess to have pure principles and who tell us to follow Jesus Christ and imitate him and have his Spirit. Let us see if they come anywhere near him and his ancient disciples. The first thing we are to look at are his precepts, of which we will mention a few. "Thou shalt love the Lord thy God with all thy heart, with all thy soul, with all thy mind, and with all thy strength. The second is like unto it. Thou shalt love thy neighbor as thyself. On these two precepts hang all the law and the prophets" (Matt. 22:37, 38, 39, 40). "By this shall all men know that they are my disciples, if ye have love one to another" (John 13:35). Our Lord left this special command with his followers, that they should love one another.

Again, John in his Epistles says, "He who loveth God loveth his brother also" (1 John 4:21). "Let us not love in word but in deed" (1 John 3:18). "Let your love be without dissimulation. See that ye love one another with a pure heart fervently" (1 Peter 1:22). "If any man say, I love God, and hateth his brother, he is a liar" (1 John 4:20). "Whosoever hateth his brother is a murderer, and no murderer hath eternal life abiding in him" [1 John 3:15]. The first thing that takes our attention is the saying of Jesus, "Thou shalt love," etc. The first question I would ask my brethren in the ministry, as well as that of the membership: What is love, or its effects? Now, if they who teach are not essentially affected with pure love, the love of God, how can they teach as they ought? Again, the holy teachers of old said, "Now if any man have not the spirit of Christ, he is none of his" (Rom. 8:9). Now, my brethren in the ministry, let me ask you a few sincere questions. Did you ever hear or read of Christ teaching his disciples that they ought to despise one because his skin was different from theirs? Jesus Christ being a Jew, and those of his Apostles certainly were not whites—and did not he who completed the plan of salvation complete it for the whites as well as for the Jews, and others? And were not the whites the most degraded people on the earth at that time? And none were more so, for they sacrificed their children to dumb idols! And did not St. Paul labor more abundantly for building up a Christian nation among you than any of the Apostles? And you know as well as I that you are not indebted to a principle beneath a white skin for your religious services but to a colored one.

What then is the matter now? Is not religion the same now under a colored skin as it ever was? If so, I would ask, why is not a man of color respected? You may say, as many say, we have white men enough. But was this the spirit of Christ and his Apostles? If it had been, there would not have been one white preacher in the world—for Jesus Christ never would have imparted his grace or word to them, for he could forever have withheld it from them. But we find that Jesus Christ and his Apostles never looked at the outward appearances. Jesus in particular looked at the hearts, and his Apostles through him, being discerners of the spirit, looked at their fruit without any regard to the skin, color, or nation; as St. Paul himself speaks, "Where there is neither Greek nor Jew, circumcision nor uncircumcision, Barbarian nor Scythian, bond nor free—but Christ is all, and in all" [Col. 3:11]. If you can find a spirit like Jesus Christ and his Apostles prevailing now in any of the white congregations, I should like to know it. I ask: Is it not the case that everybody that is not white is treated with contempt and counted as barbarians? And I ask if the word of God justifies the white man in so doing. When the prophets prophesied, of whom did they speak? When they spoke of heathens, was it not the whites and others who were counted Gentiles? And I ask if all nations with the exception of the Jews were not counted heathens.

And according to the writings of some, it could not mean the Indians, for they are counted Jews. And now I would ask: Why is all this distinction made among these Christian societies? I would ask: What is all this ado about missionary societies, if it be not to Christianize those who are not Christians? And what is it for? To degrade them worse, to bring them into society where they must welter out their days in disgrace merely because their skin is of a different complexion. What folly it is to try to make the state of human society worse than it is. How astonished some may be at this—but let me ask: Is it not so? Let me refer you to the churches only. And, my brethren, is there any agreement? Do brethren and sisters love one another? Do they not rather hate one another? Outward forms and ceremonies, the lusts of the flesh, the lusts of the eye, and pride of life is of more value to many professors than the love of God shed abroad in their hearts, or an attachment to his altar, to his ordinances, or to his children. But you may ask: Who are the children of God? Perhaps you may say, none but white. If so, the word of the Lord is not true.

I will refer you to St. Peter's precepts (Acts 10): "God is no respecter of persons," etc. Now if this is the case, my white brother, what better are you than God? And if no better, why do you, who profess his Gospel and to have his spirit, act so contrary to it? Let me ask why the men of a different skin are so despised. Why are not they educated and placed in your pulpits? I ask if his services well performed are not as good as if a white man performed them. I ask if a marriage or a funeral ceremony or the ordinance of the Lord's house would not be as acceptable in the sight of God as though he was white. And if so, why is it not to you? I ask again: Why is it not as acceptable to have men to exercise their office in one place as well as in another? Perhaps you will say that if we admit you to all of these privileges you will want more. I expect that I can guess what that is—Why, say you, there would be intermarriages. How that would be I am not able to say—and if it should be, it would be nothing strange or new to me; for I can assure you that I know a great many that have intermarried, both of the whites and the Indians—and many are their sons and daughters and people, too, of the first respectability. And I could point to some in the famous city of Boston and elsewhere. You may look now at the disgraceful act in the statute law passed by the legislature of Massachusetts, and behold the fifty-pound fine levied upon any clergyman or justice of the peace that dare to encourage the laws of God and nature by a legitimate union in holy wedlock between the Indians and whites. I would ask how this looks to your lawmakers. I would ask if this corresponds with your sayings—that you think as much of the Indians as you do of the whites. I do not wonder that you blush, many of you, while you read; for many have broken the ill-fated laws made by man to hedge up the laws of God and nature. I would ask if they who have made the law have not broken it—but there is no other state in New England that has this law but Massachusetts; and I think, as many of you do not, that you have done yourselves no credit.

But as I am not looking for a wife, having one of the finest cast, as you no doubt would understand while you read her experience and travail of soul in the way to heaven, you will see that it is not my object. And if I had none, I should not want anyone to take my right from me and choose a wife for me; for I think that I or any of my brethren have a right to choose a wife for themselves as well as the whites—and as the whites have taken the liberty to choose my brethren, the Indians, hundreds and thousands of them, as partners in life, I believe the Indians have as much right to choose their partners among the whites if they wish. I would ask you if you can see anything inconsistent in your conduct and talk about the Indians. And if you do, I hope you will try to become more consistent. Now, if the Lord Jesus Christ, who is counted by all to be a Jew—and it is well known that the Jews are a colored people, especially those living in the East, where Christ was born—and if he should appear among us, would he not be shut out of doors by many, very quickly? And by those too who profess religion?

By what you read, you may learn how deep your principles are. I should say they were skin-deep. I should not wonder if some of the most selfish and ignorant would spout a charge of their principles now and then at me. But I would ask: How are you to love your neighbors as yourself? Is it to cheat them? Is it to wrong them in anything? Now, to cheat them out of any of their rights is robbery. And I ask: Can you deny that you are not robbing the Indians daily, and many others? But at last you may think I am what is called a hard and uncharitable man. But not so. I believe there are many who would not hesitate to advocate our cause; and those too who are men of fame and respectability—as well as ladies of honor and virtue. There is a Webster, an Everett, and a Wirt, and many others who are distinguished characters—besides a host of my fellow citizens, who advocate our cause daily. And how I congratulate such noble spirits—how they are to be prized and valued; for they are well calculated to promote the happiness of mankind. They well know that man was made for society, and not for hissing-stocks and outcasts. And when such a principle as this lies within the hearts of men, how much it is like its God—and how it honors its Maker—and how it imitates the feelings of the Good Samaritan, that had his wounds bound up, who had been among thieves and robbers.

Do not get tired, ye noble-hearted—only think how many poor Indians want their wounds done up daily; the Lord will reward you, and pray you stop not till this tree of distinction shall be leveled to the earth, and the mantle of prejudice torn from every American heart—then shall peace pervade the Union.

William Apess[16]

16. In the 1837 edition, *Experience of Five Christian Indians*, Apess removed this entire essay and substituted the following (entitled "An Indian's Thought") in its place and thus ended the book: "He would ask the white Christian thus: How can you let your light shine among Indians unless you do it by example? Proof of the Savior's light. Not by precept only, that he loved the world, but by example. Such as doing all manner of cures, by working miracles, to the astonishment of all the world; and to test his love for them, he laid down his life for them, even while they were enemies. Now, if we have his spirit, as we profess to have, we shall most certainly want the indigent of all classes made comfortable. And who that understands the history of the world, does not know that ignorance is the cause of the major part of the vices that exist in the world. Now, does not the white man know that it is his duty to educate the Indians, to help them build houses of worship, and such like, in order to raise them up and make them comfortable as yourselves? And do you not know it was the intent of Christ's dying to make you and them equal with himself in holiness and peace? Now, this is just the way you ought to feel toward all the race of mankind. And you can never make ignorant people know that you love them, unless you do something for them. And be it known to all men, that your light can never shine unless you do it by works of righteousness. Judge ye, what that is.—William Apess"

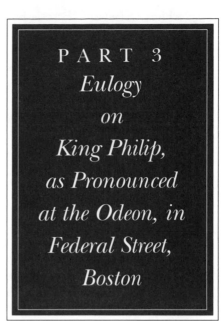

PART 3

Eulogy

on

King Philip,

as Pronounced

at the Odeon, in

Federal Street,

Boston

The *Eulogy on King Philip* was delivered twice, the first time on January 8 and the second on January 26, in a shortened version. The reasons for its being repeated can only be surmised from the text of the newspaper notices that announced it, promising "his full view of the mission cause, as there was some dissatisfaction at the previous one at the Odeon." It is clear that he was asked to repeat the address, though there is no indication of any sponsorship of the first address. We can guess that Apess meant, if no one else did, to observe the 160th anniversary of Philip's death and thus to honor him. It may have pleased him that he was still able to generate controversy, and especially around what had for almost ten years been the focus of his speaking and writing. Apess had long been unsparing about the falsity of "Christian" missionaries to the Indians who shamed and humiliated those to whom they had supposedly come in the name of Christ, a savior, as Apess liked to remind people, who was himself not white and whose salvation was for all, no matter their color, class, gender, or nationality. He condemned not only the most egregious behavior of those ministers who assisted or directly joined in land deals at the expense of Native Americans but also the mistaking of Christianity as an instrument of Euro-American notions of what constituted civilization.

The main body of the speech concentrates on a detailed account, with Philip at its center, of the early history of the encounters between New England Native Americans and the English. The attention to detail and the insistence on recalling this history can be seen in Apess's earlier writing, especially, of course, in his inclusion of the Appendix to *A Son of the Forest*. Unlike the Appendix, however, the *Eulogy* concerns itself only with New England history, although Apess is careful to insist that the treatment by whites of Indians there is symptomatic of the pattern everywhere in the United States. The best modern histories of the encounters between New England Native Americans and the Anglo-Americans confirm the interpretative stance Apess takes. Accurate though it is, Apess always deploys this history to move his larger indictment of white culture and his insistence that its destructiveness will eventually turn back on its progenitors.

In choosing Philip and early New England Anglo-Indian history as his emphasis, Apess had some precedent. Some Anglo-American writers had already provided portraits of these years that were sympathetic to the Indians, damned the Pilgrims and Puritans, and portrayed Philip as a noble and tragic hero. The difference has to do with Apess's insistence on giving this history a contemporary resonance, connecting the past treatment of Indians to present policy and calling for change. For him, history was to be not an excuse for nostalgia or vain regret but an accounting of what had been and what might yet be done differently.

These two occasions were his last in the public eye. And the *Eulogy* was his final publication of himself to a society that briefly noticed and then forgot him.

I do not arise to spread before you the fame of a noted warrior, whose natural abilities shone like those of the great and mighty Philip of Greece, or of Alexander the Great, or like those of Washington—whose virtues and patriotism are engraven on the hearts of my audience. Neither do I approve of war as being the best method of bowing to the haughty tyrant, Man, and civilizing the world. No, far from me be such a thought. But it is to bring before you beings made by the God of Nature, and in whose hearts and heads he has planted sympathies that shall live forever in the memory of the world, whose brilliant talents shone in the display of natural things, so that the most cultivated, whose powers shown with equal luster, were not able to prepare mantles to cover the burning elements of an uncivilized world. What, then? Shall we cease to mention the mighty of the earth, the noble work of God?

Yet those purer virtues remain untold. Those noble traits that marked the wild man's course lie buried in the shades of night; and who shall stand? I appeal to the lovers of liberty. But those few remaining descendants who now remain as the monument of the cruelty of those who came to improve our race and correct our errors—and as the immortal Washington lives endeared and engraven on the hearts of every white in America, never to be forgotten in time—even such is the immortal Philip honored, as held in memory by the degraded but yet grateful descendants who appreciate his character; so will every patriot, especially in this enlightened age, respect the rude yet all-accomplished son of the forest, that died a martyr to his cause, though unsuccessful, yet as glorious as the *American* Revolution. Where, then, shall we place the hero of the wilderness?

Justice and humanity for the remaining few prompt me to vindicate the character of him who yet lives in their hearts and, if possible, melt the prejudice that exists in the hearts of those who are in the possession of his soil, and only by the right of conquest—is the aim of him who proudly tells you, the blood of a denominated savage runs in his veins. It is, however, true that there are many who are said to be honorable warriors, who, in the wisdom of their civilized legislation, think it no crime to wreak their vengeance upon whole nations and communities, until the fields are covered with blood and the rivers turned into purple fountains, while groans, like distant thunder, are heard from the wounded and the tens of thousands of the dying, leaving helpless families depending on their cares and sympathies for life; while a loud response is heard floating through the air from the ten thousand Indian children and orphans, who are left to mourn the honorable acts of a few—civilized men.

Now, if we have common sense and ability to allow the difference between the civilized and the uncivilized, we cannot but see that one mode of warfare is as just as the other; for while one is sanctioned by authority of the enlightened and cultivated men, the other is an agreement according to the pure laws of nature, growing out of natural consequences; for nature always has her defense for every beast of the field; even the reptiles of the earth and the fishes of the sea have their weapons of war. But though frail man was made for a nobler purpose—to live, to love, and adore his God, and do good to his brother—for this reason, and this alone, the God of heaven prepared ways and means to blast anger, man's destroyer, and cause the Prince of Peace to rule, that man might swell those blessed notes. My image is of God; I am not a beast.

But as all men are governed by animal passions who are void of the true principles of God, whether cultivated or uncultivated, we shall now lay before you the true character of Philip, in relation to those hostilities between himself and the whites; and in so doing, permit me to be plain and candid.

The first inquiry is: Who is Philip? He was the descendant of one of the most celebrated chiefs in the known world, for peace and universal benevolence toward all men;[1] for injuries upon injuries, and the most daring robberies and barbarous deeds of death that were ever committed by the American Pilgrims, were with patience and resignation borne, in a manner that would do justice to any Christian nation or being in the world—especially when we realize that it was voluntary suffering on the part of the good old chief. His country extensive, his men numerous, so as the wilderness was enlivened by them, say, a thousand to one of the white men, and they also sick and feeble—where, then, shall we find one nation submitting so tamely to another, with such a host at their command? For injuries of much less magnitude have the people called Christians slain their brethren, till they could sing, like Samson: With a jawbone of an ass have we slain our thousands and laid them in

---

1. Philip's father was the Pokanoket sachem Massasoit who, as the rest of the *Eulogy* makes clear, became the Pilgrims' crucial ally.

heaps. It will be well for us to lay those deeds and depredations committed by whites upon Indians before the civilized world, and then they can judge for themselves.

It appears from history that, in 1614, "There came one Henry Harly unto me, bringing with him a native of the Island of Capawick [Chappaquid-dick], a place at the south of Cape Cod, whose name was Epenuel. This man was taken upon the main by force, with some twenty-nine others," very probably good old Massasoit's men (see Harlow's Voyage, 1611),[2] "by a ship, and carried to London, and from thence to be sold for slaves among the Spaniards; but the Indians being too shrewd, or, as they say, unapt for their use, they refused to traffic in Indians' blood and bones." This inhuman act of the whites caused the Indians to be jealous forever afterward, which the white man acknowledges upon the first pages of the history of his country. (See Drake's *History of the Indians*, 7.)

How inhuman it was in those wretches, to come into a country where nature shone in beauty, spreading her wings over the vast continent, shelter-ing beneath her shades those natural sons of an Almighty Being, that shone in grandeur and luster like the stars of the first magnitude in the heavenly world; whose virtues far surpassed their more enlightened foes, notwith-standing their pretended zeal for religion and virtue. How they could go to work to enslave a free people and call it religion is beyond the power of my imagination and outstrips the revelation of God's word. O thou pretended hypocritical Christian, whoever thou art, to say it was the design of God that we should murder and slay one another because we have the power. Power was not given us to abuse each other, but a mere power delegated to us by the King of heaven, a weapon of defense against error and evil; and when abused, it will turn to our destruction. Mark, then, the history of nations throughout the world.

But notwithstanding the transgression of this power to destroy the In-dians at their first discovery, yet it does appear that the Indians had a wish to

---

2. Apess's own notes will appear throughout this text within parentheses. He seems to have confused Thomas Hunt's 1614 capture of about twenty Indians for sale as slaves with the exploits of Edward Harlow. Whereas Hunt tried unsuccessfully to sell his captives in Spain, Harlow commanded an expedition in 1611 to kidnap Indians for the purpose of making them guides for the English. Among those Harlow captured was Epenow (Epenuel), a sachem from Martha's Vineyard. Epenow spent three years with Sir Ferdinando Gorges, the commander of the Plymouth fort in England who had an interest in colonizing New England. He told Gorges stories of fabulous gold mines. In 1614 Gorges sent an expedition back to find the mines, only to have Epenow leap overboard as the ship approached the island. Epenow's countrymen assisted him by showering the boat with a barrage of arrows, wounding the captain and a number of his crew. From Neal Salisbury, *Manitou and Providence: Indians, Europeans, and the Making of New England, 1500–1643* (New York: Oxford University Press, 1982), 95.

be friendly. When the Pilgrims came among them (Iyanough's men),[3] there appeared an old woman, breaking out in solemn lamentations, declaring one Captain Hunt had carried off three of her children, and they would never return here. The Pilgrims replied that they were bad and wicked men, but they were going to do better and would never injure them at all. And, to pay the poor mother, gave her a few brass trinkets, to atone for her three sons and appease her present feelings, a woman nearly one hundred years of age. O white woman! What would you think if some foreign nation, unknown to you, should come and carry away from you three lovely children, whom you had dandled on the knee, and at some future time you should behold them and break forth in sorrow, with your heart broken, and merely ask, "Sirs, where are my little ones?" and some one should reply: "It was passion, great passion." What would you think of them? Should you not think they were beings made more like rocks than men? Yet these same men came to these Indians for support and acknowledge themselves that no people could be used better than they were; that their treatment would do honor to any nation; that their provisions were in abundance; that they gave them venison and sold them many hogsheads of corn to fill their stores, besides beans. This was in the year 1622. Had it not been for this humane act of the Indians, every white man would have been swept from the New England colonies. In their sickness, too, the Indians were as tender to them as to their own children; and for all this, they were denounced as savages by those who had received all the acts of kindness they possibly could show them. After these social acts of the Indians toward those who were suffering, and those of their countrymen, who well knew the care their brethren had received by them—how were the Indians treated before that? Oh, hear! In the following manner, and their own words, we presume, they will not deny.

December (O.S.)[4] 1620, the Pilgrims landed at Plymouth, and without asking liberty from anyone they possessed themselves of a portion of the country, and built themselves houses, and then made a treaty, and commanded them to accede to it. This, if now done, it would be called an insult, and every white man would be called to go out and act the part of a patriot, to defend their country's rights; and if every intruder were butchered, it would be sung upon every hilltop in the Union that victory and patriotism was the order of the day. And yet the Indians (though many were dissatisfied), without the shedding of blood or imprisoning anyone, bore it. And yet for their

3. Iyanough of Cummaquid was one of the sachems who were counted as allies of the Plymouth colony until Miles Standish lashed out against a "conspiracy" of Massachusett leaders in 1623, killing seven. From Salisbury, *Manitou and Providence*, 130–34.
4. Old Style. Dates were ten days earlier than they would be currently.

kindness and resignation toward the whites, they were called savages and made by God on purpose for them to destroy. We might say, God understood his work better than this. But to proceed: It appears that a treaty was made by the Pilgrims and the Indians, which treaty was kept during forty years; the young chiefs during this time was showing the Pilgrims how to live in their country and find support for their wives and little ones; and for all this, they were receiving the applause of being savages. The two gentleman chiefs were Squanto and Samoset, that were so good to the Pilgrims.[5]

The next we present before you are things very appalling. We turn our attention to the dates 1623, January and March, when Mr. Weston's colony came very near starving to death; some of them were obliged to hire themselves to the Indians, to become their servants, in order that they might live.[6] Their principal work was to bring wood and water; but, not being contented with this, many of the whites sought to steal the Indians' corn; and because the Indians complained of it, and through their complaint, some one of their number being punished, as they say, to appease the savages. Now let us see who the greatest savages were; the person that stole the corn was a stout athletic man, and because of this they wished to spare him and take an old man who was lame and sickly and that used to get his living by weaving, and because they thought he would not be of so much use to them, he was, although innocent of any crime, hung in his stead. O savage, where art thou, to weep over the Christian's crimes? Another act of humanity for Christians, as they call themselves, that one Captain Standish, gathering some fruit and provisions, goes forward with a black and hypocritical heart and pretends to prepare a feast for the Indians; and when they sit down to eat, they seize the Indians' knives hanging about their necks, and stab them to the heart. The white people call this stabbing, feasting the savages. We suppose it might well mean themselves, their conduct being more like savages than Christians. They took one Wittumumet,[7] the chief's head, and put it upon a pole in their fort and, for aught we know, gave praise to their God for success in murdering

---

5. Samoset, an Abenaki whose people had experience trading with the English, and Squanto, a well-traveled captive who had been taken to England at one time, arranged for the March 1621 meeting between the Pokanoket and the English that resulted in a treaty. The treaty, in addition to symbolizing the mutual good will between the Pokanoket and the colonizers, freed Squanto to live with the English, whom he served as an interpreter, guide, and diplomat. From Salisbury, *Manitou and Providence*, 114–16.

6. Thomas Weston, a non-Separatist London merchant, formed a second colony in 1622 at Wessagusset, north of the Plymouth colony, consisting of sixty single men, most of whom had arrived earlier at Plymouth without adequate provisions. Ibid., 125.

7. Wituwament, a Massachusett sachem, was lured into an English home and killed with his own knife as part of Standish's preventive attacks to frustrate the Massachusett "conspiracy." Ibid., 130.

a poor Indian; for we know it was their usual course to give praise to God for this kind of victory, believing it was God's will and command for them to do so. We wonder if these same Christians do not think it the command of God that they should lie, steal, and get drunk, commit fornication and adultery. The one is as consistent as the other. What say you, judges, is it not so, and was it not according as they did? Indians think it is.

But we will proceed to show another inhuman act. The whites robbed the Indian graves, and their corn, about the year 1632, which caused Chicataubut to be displeased, who was chief, and also a son to the woman that was dead.[8] And according to the Indian custom, it was a righteous act to be avenged of the dead. Accordingly, he called all his men together and addressed them thus: "When last the glorious light of the sky was underneath this globe, and birds grew silent, I began to settle, as is my custom, to take repose. Before my eyes were fast closed, methought I saw a vision, at which my spirit was much troubled. A spirit cried aloud, 'Behold, my son, whom I have cherished, see the paps that gave thee suck, the hands that clasped thee warm, and fed thee oft. Can thou forget to take revenge of those wild people that have my monument defaced in a despiteful manner, disdaining our ancient antiquities and honorable customs? See, now, the sachem's grave lies, like unto the common people of ignoble race, defaced. Thy mother doth complain and implores thy aid against these thievish people, now come hither. If this be suffered, I shall not rest quiet within my everlasting habitation.'" War was the result. And where is there a people in the world that would see their friends robbed of their common property, their nearest and dearest friends; robbed, after their last respects to them? I appeal to you, who value your friends and affectionate mothers, if you would have robbed them of their fine marble, and your storehouses broken open, without calling those to account who did it. I trust not; and if another nation should come to these regions and begin to rob and plunder all that came in their way, would not the orators of the day be called to address the people and arouse them to war for such insults? And, for all this, would they not be called Christians and patriots? Yes, it would be rung from Georgia to Maine, from the ocean to the lakes, what fine men and Christians there were in the land. But when a few red children attempt to defend their rights, they are condemned as savages by those, if possible, who have indulged in wrongs more cruel than the Indians.

But there is still more. In 1619 a number of Indians went on board of a ship, by order of their chief, and the whites set upon them and murdered them without mercy; says Mr. Dermer, "without the Indians giving them the least provocation whatever."[9] Is this insult to be borne, and not a word to be

8. A Massachusett who led a band of fifty to sixty followers. Ibid., 184.

9. Captain Thomas Dermer led expeditions to New England on behalf of Ferdinando Gorges in

said? Truly, Christians would never bear it; why, then, think it strange that the denominated savages do not? O thou white Christian, look at acts that honored your countrymen, to the destruction of thousands, for much less insults than that. And who, my dear sirs, were wanting of the name of savages—whites, or Indians? Let justice answer.

But we have more to present; and that is the violation of a treaty that the Pilgrims proposed for the Indians to subscribe to, and they the first to break it. The Pilgrims promised to deliver up every transgressor of the Indian treaty to them, to be punished according to their laws, and the Indians were to do likewise. Now it appears that an Indian had committed treason by conspiring against the king's life, which is punishable with death; and Massasoit makes demand for the transgressor, and the Pilgrims refuse to give him up, although by their oath of alliance they had promised to do so.[10] Their reasons were, he was beneficial to them. This shows how grateful they were to their former safeguard and ancient protector. Now, who would have blamed this venerable old chief if he had declared war at once and swept the whole colonies away? It was certainly in his power to do it, if he pleased; but no, he forbore and forgave the whites. But where is there a people, called civilized, that would do it? We presume, none; and we doubt not but the Pilgrims would have exerted all their powers to be avenged and to appease their ungodly passions. But it will be seen that this good old chief exercised more Christian forbearance than any of the governors of that age or since. It might well be said he was a pattern for the Christians themselves; but by the Pilgrims he is denounced, as being a savage.

It does not appear that Massasoit or his sons were respected because they were human beings but because they feared him; and we are led to believe that, if it had been in the power of the Pilgrims, they would have butchered them out and out, notwithstanding all the piety they professed.

Only look for a few moments at the abuses the son of Massasoit received. Alexander being sent for with armed men, and while he and his men were breaking their fast in the morning, they were taken immediately away, by order of the governor, without the least provocation but merely through suspicion.[11] Alexander and his men saw them and might have prevented it but did not, saying the governor had no occasion to treat him in this manner;

1619 and 1620. The incident Dermer recounted occurred in the summer of 1620 when an English crew coasting along Massachusetts Bay invited some Pokanokets onto the ship and then murdered them.

10. This passage refers to Squanto, who plotted against Massasoit but was protected by the Pilgrims, who needed his aid.

11. Alexander was the eldest son of Massasoit and Philip's brother. Apess's account captures what seems actually to have occurred.

and the heartless wretch informed him that he would murder him upon the spot if he did not go with him, presenting a sword at his breast; and had it not been for one of his men he would have yielded himself up upon the spot. Alexander was a man of strong passion and of a firm mind; and this insulting treatment of him caused him to fall sick of a fever, so that he never recovered. Some of the Indians were suspicious that he was poisoned to death. He died in the year 1662. "After him," says that eminent divine, Dr. Mather,[12] "there rose up one Philip, of cursed memory." Perhaps if the Doctor was present, he would find that the memory of Philip was as far before his, in the view of sound, judicious men, as the sun is before the stars at noonday. But we might suppose that men like Dr. Mather, so well versed in Scripture, would have known his work better than to have spoken evil of anyone, or have cursed any of God's works. He ought to have known that God did not make his red children for him to curse; but if he wanted them cursed, he could have done it himself. But, on the contrary, his suffering Master commanded him to love his enemies and to pray for his persecutors, and to do unto others as he would that men should do unto him. Now, we wonder if the sons of the Pilgrims would like to have us, poor Indians, come out and curse the Doctor, and all their sons, as we have been by many of them. And suppose that, in some future day, our children should repay all these wrongs, would it not be doing as we, poor Indians, have been done to? But we sincerely hope there is more humanity in us than that.

In the history of Massasoit we find that his own head men were not satisfied with the Pilgrims, that they looked upon them to be intruders and had a wish to expel those intruders out of their coast; and no wonder that from the least reports the Pilgrims were ready to take it up. A false report was made respecting one Tisquantum, that he was murdered by an Indian, one of Coubantant's men.[13] Upon this news, one Standish, a vile and malicious fellow, took fourteen of his lewd Pilgrims with him, and at midnight, when a deathless silence reigned throughout the wilderness; not even a bird is heard to send forth her sweet songs to charm and comfort those children of the woods; but all had taken their rest, to commence anew on the rising of the glorious sun. But to their sad surprise there was no rest for them, but they were surrounded by ruffians and assassins; yes, assassins, what better name can be given them? At that late hour of the night, meeting a house in the wilderness, whose inmates were nothing but a few helpless females and children; soon a voice is heard—"Move not, upon the peril of your life." I

12. This is Increase Mather, Cotton Mather's father. Both wrote virulently against Indians, but it was Increase Mather who wrote most at length on King Philip's War.

13. Tisquantum was another name for Squanto. Coubantant was a sachem at Nemasket who had kidnapped Squanto and another of Plymouth's Indian advisers in August 1621.

appeal to this audience if there was any righteousness in their proceedings. Justice would say no. At the same time some of the females were so frightened that some of them undertook to make their escape, upon which they were fired upon. Now, it is doubtless the case that these females never saw a white man before, or ever heard a gun fired. It must have sounded to them like the rumbling of thunder, and terror must certainly have filled all their hearts. And can it be supposed that these innocent Indians could have looked upon them as good and trusty men? Do you look upon the midnight robber and assassin as being a Christian and trusty man? These Indians had not done one single wrong act to the whites but were as innocent of any crime as any beings in the world. And do you believe that Indians cannot feel and see, as well as white people? If you think so, you are mistaken. Their power of feeling and knowing is as quick as yours. Now this is to be borne, as the Pilgrims did as their Master told them to; but what color he was I leave it. But if the real sufferers say one word, they are denounced as being wild and savage beasts.

But let us look a little further. It appears that in 1630 a benevolent chief bid the Pilgrims welcome to his shores and, in June 28, 1630, ceded his land to them for the small sum of eighty dollars, now Ipswich, Rowley, and a part of Essex.[14] The following year, at the July term, 1631, these Pilgrims of the New World passed an act in court, that the friendly chief should not come into their houses short of paying fifty dollars or an equivalent, that is, ten beaver skins. Who could have supposed that the meek and lowly followers of virtue would have taken such methods to rob honest men of the woods? But, for this insult, the Pilgrims had well-nigh lost the lives and their all, had it not been prevented by Robbin, an Indian, who apprised them of their danger. And now let it be understood, notwithstanding all the bitter feelings the whites have generally shown toward Indians, yet they have been the only instrument in preserving their lives.

The history of New England writers say that our tribes were large and respectable. How, then, could it be otherwise, but their safety rested in the hands of friendly Indians? In 1647, the Pilgrims speak of large and respectable tribes. But let us trace them for a few moments. How have they been destroyed? Is it by fair means? No. How then? By hypocritical proceedings, by being duped and flattered; flattered by informing the Indians that their God was a going to speak to them, and then place them before the cannon's mouth in a line, and then putting the match to it and kill thousands of them. We might suppose that meek Christians had better gods and weapons than cannon; weapons that were not carnal, but mighty through God, to the

14. This is Masconomo, and the "Pilgrims" he is welcoming were actually the Puritans of the Massachusetts Bay Colony, whose governor was John Winthrop.

pulling down of strongholds. These are the weapons that modern Christians profess to have; and if the Pilgrims did not have them, they ought not to be honored as such. But let us again review their weapons to civilize the nations of this soil. What were they? Rum and powder and ball, together with all the diseases, such as the smallpox and every other disease imaginable, and in this way sweep off thousands and tens of thousands. And then it has been said that these men who were free from these things, that they could not live among civilized people. We wonder how a virtuous people could live in a sink of diseases, a people who had never been used to them.

And who is to account for those destructions upon innocent families and helpless children? It was said by some of the New England writers that living babes were found at the breast of their dead mothers. What an awful sight! And to think, too, that these diseases were carried among them on purpose to destroy them. Let the children of the Pilgrims blush, while the son of the forest drops a tear and groans over the fate of his murdered and departed fathers. He would say to the sons of the Pilgrims (as Job said about his birthday), let the day be dark, the 22nd day of December 1622;[15] let it be forgotten in your celebration, in your speeches, and by the burying of the rock that your fathers first put their foot upon. For be it remembered, although the Gospel is said to be glad tidings to all people, yet we poor Indians never have found those who brought it as messengers of mercy, but contrawise. We say, therefore, let every man of color wrap himself in mourning, for the 22nd of December and the 4th of July are days of mourning and not of joy. (I would here say, there is an error in my book; it speaks of the 25th of December, but it should be the 22nd. See *Indian Nullification.*) Let them rather fast and pray to the great Spirit, the Indian's God, who deals out mercy to his red children, and not destruction.

O Christians, can you answer for those beings that have been destroyed by your hostilities, and beings too that lie endeared to God as yourselves, his Son being their Savior as well as yours, and alike to all men? And will you presume to say that you are executing the judgments of God by so doing, or as many really are approving the works of their fathers to be genuine, as it is

15. Apess, as he makes clear later in the speech, takes December 22 as the day the Pilgrims landed and stepped on Plymouth Rock. They in fact arrived in Massachusetts in December 1620. The landing at the rock is a piece of later mythology, which grew up alongside a celebration of the Founding Fathers. These twin icons in Euro-American culture each found an early and supreme articulator in Daniel Webster. Apess is, very consciously, I think, echoing and disputing Webster's reverential reading both of the "Fathers" and of the Pilgrims. The relevant speeches, among the best-known cultural expressions in Apess's day, are Webster's "First Settlement of New England" delivered at Plymouth on December 22, 1820, and his "Adams and Jefferson" delivered in Faneuil Hall, Boston, on August 2, 1826, the year the two men died on July 4—an irresistibly evocative coincidence.

certain that every time they celebrate the day of the Pilgrims they do? Although in words they deny it, yet in the works they approve of the iniquities of their fathers. And as the seed of iniquity and prejudice was sown in that day, so it still remains; and there is a deep-rooted popular opinion in the hearts of many that Indians were made, etc., on purpose for destruction, to be driven out by white Christians, and they to take their places; and that God had decreed it from all eternity. If such theologians would only study the works of nature more, they would understand the purposes of good better than they do: that the favor of the Almighty was good and holy, and all his nobler works were made to adorn his image, by being his grateful servants and admiring each other as angels, and not, as they say, to drive and devour each other. And that you may know the spirit of the Pilgrims yet remains, we will present before you the words of a humble divine of the Far West. He says, "The desert becomes an Eden." Rev. Nahum Gold, of Union Grove, Putnam, writes under the date June 12, 1835, says he, "Let any man look at this settlement, and reflect what it was three years ago, and his heart can but kindle up while he exclaims, 'what God has wrought!' the savage has left the ground for civilized man; the rich prairie, from bringing forth all its strengths to be burned, is now receiving numerous enclosures, and brings a harvest of corn and wheat to feed the church. Yes, sir, this is now God's vineyard; he has gathered the vine, the choice vine, and brought it from a far country, and has planted it on a goodly soil. He expects fruit now. He gathered out the stones thereof, and drove the red Canaanites from trampling it down, or in any way hindering its increase" (*New York Evangelist,* August 1).

But what next should we hear from this very pious man? Why, my brethren, the poor missionaries want money to go and convert the poor heathen, as if God could not convert them where they were but must first drive them out. If God wants the red men converted, we should think that he could do it as well in one place as in another. But must I say, and shall I say it, that missionaries have injured us more than they have done us good, by degrading us as a people, in breaking up our governments and leaving us without any suffrages whatever, or a legal right among men? Oh, what cursed doctrine is this! It most certainly is not fit to civilize men with, much more to save their souls; and we poor Indians want no such missionaries around us. But I would suggest one thing, and that is, let the ministers and people use the colored people they have already around them like human beings, before they go to convert any more; and let them show it in their churches; and let them proclaim it upon the housetops; and I would say to the benevolent, withhold your hard earnings from them, unless they do do it, until they can stop laying their own wickedness to God, which is blasphemy.

But if God was like his subjects, we should all have been swept off before now; for we find that, of late, Pilgrims' children have got to killing and mobbing each other, as they have got rid of most all the Indians.[16] This is worse than my countrymen ever did, for they never mobbed one another; and I was in hopes that the sons of the Pilgrims had improved a little. But the more honorable may thank their fathers for such a spirit in this age. And remember that their walls of prejudice was built with untempered mortar, contrary to God's command; and be assured, it will fall upon their children, though I sincerely hope they will not be seriously injured by it—although I myself now and then feel a little of its pressure, as though I should not be able to sustain the shock. But I trust the Great Spirit will stand by me, as also good and honorable men will, being as it were the last, still lingering upon the shores of time, standing as it were upon the graves of his much injured race, to plead their cause and speak for the rights of the remaining few. Although it is said by many that the Indians had no rights, neither do they regard their rights; nor can they look a white man in the face and ask him for them. If the white man did but know it, the Indians knows it would do no good to spend his breath for naught. But if we can trust to Roger Williams's word in regard to Indian rights: He says, no people were more so; that the cause of all their wars were about their hunting grounds. And it is certain their boundaries were set to their respective tribes; so that each one knew his own range. The poet speaks thus of Canonicus, in 1803:

> Almighty Prince, of venerable age,
> A fearless warrior, but of peace the friend;
> His breast a treasury of maxims sage,
> His arm a host, to punish or defend.[17]

It was said he was eighty-four years of age when he died, an able defender of his rights. Thus it does appear that Indians had rights, and those rights were near and dear to them, as your stores and farms and firesides are to the whites, and their wives and children also. And how the Pilgrims could rejoice at their distresses, I know not; what divinity men were made of in those days rather puzzles me now and then. Now, for example, we will lay before you the conduct of an Indian and the whites and leave you, dear sirs, to judge.

16. Mob violence, both in rural and urban areas, increased dramatically in the 1830s in the United States, reaching its peak in the summer of 1835. Anti-abolitionist mobs have been the most noticed but there were also nativist mobs attacking Catholics, anti-Mormon mobs, vigilantes lynching gamblers and others, and workingmen's mobs. Anti-abolition and anti-Negro mobs were particularly common and nowhere more so than in Massachusetts and Connecticut.

17. Canonicus was a sachem of the Narragansett who, with his nephew, Miantonomi, led the Narragansett so well that they were able to make tributary, without going to war, most of the Indian groups of the region from Narragansett Bay nearly to Boston.

History informs us that in Kennebunk there lived an Indian, remarkable for his good conduct, and who received a grant of land from the state and fixed himself in a new township, where a number of white families were settled. Though not ill treated, yet the common prejudices against Indians prevented any sympathy with him, though he himself did all that lay in his power to comfort his white neighbors, in case of sickness and death. But now let us see the scene reversed. This poor Indian, that had nourished and waited to aid the Pilgrims in their trouble, now vainly looks for help, when sickness and death comes into his family. Hear his own words. He speaks to the inhabitants thus: "When white man's child die, Indian man he sorry; he help bury him. When my child die, no one speak to me; I make his grave alone. I can no live here." He gave up his farm, dug up the body of his child, and carried it 200 miles, through the wilderness, to join the Canadian Indians. What dignity there was in this man; and we do not wonder that he felt so indignant at the proceedings of the then called Christians. But this was as they were taught by their haughty divines and orators of the day. But, nevertheless, the people were to blame, for they might have read for themselves; and they doubtless would have found that we were not made to be vessels of wrath, as they say we were. And had the whites found it out, perhaps they would not have rejoiced at a poor Indian's death or, when they were swept off, would not have called it the Lord killing the Indians to make room for them upon their lands. This is something like many people wishing for their friends to die, that they might get their property. I am astonished when I look at people's absurd blindness—when all are liable to die, and all subject to all kinds of diseases. For example, why is it that epidemics have raged so much among the more civilized? In London, 1660, the plague; and in 1830 and 1831, the cholera, in the Old and New World, when the inhabitants were lain in heaps by that epidemic. Should I hear of an Indian rejoicing over the inhabitants, I would no longer own him as a brother. But, dear friends, you know that no Indian knew by the Bible it was wrong to kill, because he knew not the Bible and its sacred laws. But it is certain the Pilgrims knew better than to break the commands of their Lord and Master; they knew that it was written, "Thou shalt not kill."

But having laid a mass of history and exposition before you, the purpose of which is to show that Philip and all the Indians generally felt indignantly toward whites, whereby they were more easily allied together by Philip, their king and emperor, we come to notice more particularly his history. As to His Majesty, King Philip, it was certain that his honor was put to the test, and it was certainly to be tried, even at the loss of his life and country. It is a matter of uncertainty about his age; but his birthplace was at Mount Hope, Rhode Island, where Massasoit, his father, lived till 1656, and died, as also his brother, Alexander, by the governor's ill-treating him (that is, Winthrop), which caused his death, as before mentioned, in 1662; after which, the kingdom fell into the hands of Philip, the greatest man that ever lived upon the American shores. Soon after his coming to the throne, it appears he began to be noticed, though, prior to this, it appears that he was not forward in the councils of war or peace. When he came into office it appears that he knew there was great responsibility resting upon himself and country, that it was likely to be ruined by those rude intruders around him, though he appears friendly and is willing to sell them lands for almost nothing, as we shall learn from dates of the Plymouth colony, which commence June 23, 1664. William Benton of Rhode Island, a merchant, buys Mattapoisett of Philip and wife, but no sum is set which he gave for it. To this deed, his counselors, and wife, and two of the Pilgrims were witnesses. In 1665 he sold New Bedford and Compton for forty dollars. In 1667 he sells to Constant Southworth and others all the meadowlands from Dartmouth to Mattapoisett, for which he received sixty dollars. The same year he sells to Thomas Willet a tract of land two miles in length and perhaps the same in width, for which he received forty dollars. In 1668 he sold a tract of some square miles, now called Swansea. The next year he sells five hundred acres in Swansea, for which he received eighty dollars. His counselors and interpreters, with the Pilgrims, were witnesses to these deeds.

Osamequan, for valuable considerations, in the year 1641 sold to John Brown and Edward Winslow a tract of land eight miles square, situated on both sides of Palmer's River. Philip, in 1668, was required to sign a quit claim of the same, which we understand he did in the presence of his counselors. In the same year Philip laid claim to a portion of land called New Meadows, alleging that it was not intended to be conveyed in a former deed, for which Mr. Brown paid him forty-four dollars, in goods; so it was settled without difficulty. Also, in 1669, for forty dollars, he sold to one John Cook a whole island called Nokatay, near Dartmouth. The same year Philip sells a tract of land in Middleborough for fifty-two dollars. In 1671 he sold to Hugh Cole a large tract of land lying near Swansea, for sixteen dollars. In 1672 he sold sixteen square miles to William Breton and others, of Taunton, for which he and his chief received five hundred and seventy-two dollars. This contract, signed by himself and chiefs, ends the sales of lands with Philip, for all which he received nine hundred and seventy-four dollars, as far as we can learn by the records.

Here Philip meets with a most bitter insult, in 1673, from one Peter Talmon of Rhode Island, who complained to the Plymouth court against Philip, of Mount Hope, predecessor, heir, and administrator of his brother Alexander, deceased, in an action on the case, to the damage of three thousand and two hundred dollars, for which the court gave verdict in favor of Talmon, the young Pilgrim; for which Philip had to make good to the said Talmon a large tract of land at Sapamet and other places adjacent. And for the want thereof, that is, more land that was not taken up, the complainant is greatly damnified. This is the language in the Pilgrims' court. Now let us review this a little. The man who bought this land made the contract, as he says, with Alexander, ten or twelve years before; then why did he not bring forward his contract before the court? It is easy to understand why he did not. Their object was to cheat, or get the whole back again in this way. Only look at the sum demanded, and it is enough to satisfy the critical observer. This course of proceedings caused the chief and his people to entertain strong jealousies of the whites.

In the year 1668 Philip made a complaint against one Weston, who had wronged one of his men of a gun and some swine; and we have no account that he got any justice for his injured brethren. And, indeed, it would be a strange thing for poor unfortunate Indians to find justice in those courts of the pretended pious in those days, or even since; and for a proof of my assertion I will refer the reader or hearer to the records of legislatures and courts throughout New England, and also to my book, *Indian Nullification*.

We would remark still further: Who stood up in those days, and since, to plead Indian rights? Was it the friend of the Indian? No, it was his enemies who rose—his enemies, to judge and pass sentence. And we know that such kind of characters as the Pilgrims were, in regard to the Indians' rights, who, as they say, had none, must certainly always give verdict against them, as, generally speaking, they always have. Prior to this insult, it appears that Philip had met with great difficulty with the Pilgrims, that they appeared to be suspicious of him in 1671; and the Pilgrims sent for him, but he did not appear to move as though he cared much for their messenger, which caused them to be still more suspicious. What grounds the Pilgrims had is not ascertained, unless it is attributed to a guilty conscience for wrongs done to Indians. It appears that Philip, when he got ready, goes near to them and sends messengers to Taunton, to invite the Pilgrims to come and treat with him; but the governor, being either too proud or afraid, sends messengers to him to come to their residence at Taunton, to which he complied. Among these messengers was the Honorable Roger Williams, a Christian and a patriot and a friend to the Indians, for which we rejoice. Philip, not liking to trust the Pilgrims, left some of the whites in his stead to warrant his safe return. When Philip and his men had come near the place, some of the Plymouth people were ready to attack him; this rashness was, however, prevented by the commissioner of Massachusetts, who met there with the governor to treat with Philip; and it was agreed upon to meet in the meetinghouse.

Philip's complaint was that the Pilgrims had injured the planting grounds of his people. The Pilgrims, acting as umpires, say the charges against them were not sustained; and because it was not, to their satisfaction, the whites wanted that Philip should order all his men to bring in his arms and ammunition; and the court was to dispose of them as they pleased. The next thing was that Philip must pay the cost of the treaty, which was four hundred dollars. The pious Dr. Mather says that Philip was appointed to pay a sum of money to defray the charges that his insolent clamors had put the colony to. We wonder if the Pilgrims were as ready to pay the Indians for the trouble they put them to. If they were, it was with the instruments of death. It appears that Philip did not wish to make war with them but compromised with them; and in order to appease the Pilgrims he actually did order his men, whom he could not trust, to deliver them up; but his own men withheld, with the exception of a very few.

Now, what an unrighteous act this was in the people who professed to be friendly and humane and peaceable to all men. It could not be that they were so devoid of sense as to think these illiberal acts would produce peace but, contrawise, continual broils. And, in fact, it does appear that they courted war instead of peace, as it appears from a second council that was held by order of the governor, at Plymouth, September 13, 1671. It appears that they sent again for Philip; but he did not attend but went himself and made complaint to the governor, which made him write to the council and ordered them to desist, to be more mild, and not to take such rash measures. But it appears that on the 24th the scene changed, that they held another council; and the disturbers of the peace, the intruders upon a peaceable people, say they find Philip guilty of the following charges:

1. That he had neglected to bring in his arms, although competent time had been given him.
2. That he had carried insolently and proudly toward us on several occasions, in refusing to come down to our courts (when sent for), to procure a right understanding betwixt us.

What an insult this was to His Majesty; an independent chief of a powerful nation should come at the beck and call of his neighbors whenever they pleased to have him do it. Besides, did not Philip do as he agreed, at Taunton? That is, in case there was more difficulty they were to leave it to Massachusetts, to be settled there in the high council, and both parties were to abide by their decision—but did the Pilgrims wait? No. But being infallible, of course they could not err.

The third charge was: harboring divers Indians, not his own men but the vagabond Indians.

Now, what a charge this was to bring against a king, calling his company vagabonds, because it did not happen to please them; and what right had they to find fault with his company? I do not believe that Philip ever troubled himself about the white people's company and prefer charges against them for keeping company with whom they pleased. Neither do I believe he called their company vagabonds, for he was more noble than that.

The fourth charge is that he went to Massachusetts with his council and complained against them and turned their brethren against them.

This was more a complaint against themselves than Philip, inasmuch as it represents that Philip's story was so correct that they were blamable.

5. That he had not been quite so civil as they wished him to be.

We presume that Philip felt himself much troubled by these intruders and of course put them off from time to time, or did not take much notice of their proposals. Now, such charges as those, we think, are to no credit of the Pilgrims. However, this council ended much as the other did, in regard to disarming the Indians, which they never were able to do. Thus ended the events of 1671.

But it appears that the Pilgrims could not be contented with what they had done, but they must send an Indian, and a traitor, to preach to Philip and his men, in order to convert him and his people to Christianity. The preacher's name was Sassamon. I would appeal to this audience: Is it not certain that the Plymouth people strove to pick a quarrel with Philip and his men? What could have been more insulting than to send a man to them who was false, and looked upon as such? For it is most certain that a traitor was, above all others, the more to be detested than any other. And not only so; it was the laws of the Indians that such a man must die, that he had forfeited his life; and when he made his appearance among them, Philip would have killed him upon the spot if his council had not persuaded him not to. But it appears that in March 1674 one of Philip's men killed him and placed him beneath the ice in a certain pond near Plymouth, doubtless by the order of Philip. After this, search was made for him, and they found there a certain Indian, by the name of Patuckson; Tobias, also, his son, were apprehended and tried. Tobias was one of Philip's counselors, as it appears from the records that the trial did not end here, that it was put over, and that two of the Indians entered into bonds for $400, for the appearance of Tobias at the June term, for which a mortgage of land was taken to that amount for his safe return. June having arrived, three instead of one are arraigned. There was no one but Tobias suspected at the previous court. Now two others are arraigned, tried, condemned, and executed (making three in all) in June the 8th, 1675, by hanging and shooting. It does not appear that any more than one was guilty, and it was said that he was known to acknowledge it; but the other two persisted in their innocence to the last.

This murder of the preacher brought on the war a year sooner than it was anticipated by Philip. But this so exasperated King Philip that from that day he studied to be revenged of the Pilgrims, judging that his white intruders had nothing to do in punishing his people for any crime and that it was in violation of treaties of ancient date. But when we look at this, how bold and how daring it was to Philip, as though they would bid defiance to him, and all his authority; we do not wonder at his exasperation. When the governor finds that His Majesty was displeased, he then sends messengers to him and wishes to know why he would make war upon him (as if he had done all right), and wished to enter into a new treaty with him. The king answered them thus: "Your governor is but a subject of King Charles of England; I shall not treat with a subject; I shall treat of peace only with a king, my brother; when he comes, I am ready."

This answer of Philip's to the messengers is worthy of note throughout the world. And never could a prince answer with more dignity in regard to his official authority than he did—disdaining the idea of placing himself upon a par of the minor subjects of a king; letting them know, at the same time, that he felt his independence more than they thought he did. And indeed it was time for him to wake up, for now the subjects of King Charles had taken one of his counselors and killed him, and he could no longer trust them. Until the execution of these three Indians, supposed to be the murderers of Sassamon, no hostility was committed by Philip or his warriors. About the time of their trial, he was said to be marching his men up and down the country in arms; but when it was known, he could no longer restrain his young men, who, upon the 24th of June [1675], provoked the people of Swansea by killing their cattle and other injuries, which was a signal to commence the war, and what they had desired, as a superstitious notion prevailed among the Indians that whoever fired the first gun of either party would be conquered, doubtless a notion they had received from the Pilgrims. It was upon a fast day, too, when the first gun was fired; and as the people were returning from church, they were fired upon by the Indians, when several of them were killed. It is not supposed that Philip directed this attack but was opposed to it. Though it is not doubted that he meant to be revenged upon his enemies; for during some time he had been cementing his countrymen together, as it appears that he had sent to all the disaffected tribes, who also had watched the movements of the comers from the New World[18] and were as dissatisfied as Philip himself was with their proceedings.

18. His "comers from the New World" may only be a slip of the pen, referring as he is to the Europeans, who are conventionally, of course, from the "Old" World, having "discovered" the

Now around the council fires they met,
    The young nobles for to greet;
Their tales of woe and sorrows to relate,
    About the Pilgrims, their wretched foes.

And while their fires were blazing high,
    Their king and Emperor to greet;
His voice like lightning fires their hearts,
    To stand the test or die.

See those Pilgrims from the world unknown,
    No love for Indians do know:
Although our fathers fed them well
    With venison rich, of precious kinds.

No gratitude to Indians now is shown,
    From people saved by them alone;
All gratitude that poor Indian do know,
    Is, we are robbed of all our rights.[19]

At this council it appears that Philip made the following speech to his chiefs, counselors, and warriors:

Brothers, you see this vast country before us, which the Great Spirit gave to our fathers and us; you see the buffalo and deer that now are our support. Brothers, you see these little ones, our wives and children, who are looking to us for food and raiment; and you now see the foe before you, that they have grown insolent and bold; that all our ancient customs are disregarded; the treaties made by our fathers and us are broken, and all of us insulted; our council fires disregarded, and all the ancient customs of our fathers; our brothers murdered before our eyes, and their spirits cry to us for revenge. Brothers, these people from the unknown world will cut down our groves, spoil our hunting and planting grounds, and drive us and our children from the graves of our fathers, and our council fires, and enslave our women and children.

This famous speech of Philip was calculated to arouse them to arms, to do the best they could in protecting and defending their rights. The blow had now been struck, the die was cast, and nothing but blood and carnage was

"New." This is, however, so like Apess's wit and his delight in inverting the conventions of language through which Europeans validated their presence and their dominance in the Americas that it may be entirely deliberate—for the Europeans were of course from a new world from the perspective of Native Americans.

19. I have not been able to identify this poem.

before them. And we find Philip as active as the wind, as dexterous as a giant, firm as the pillows of heaven, and fierce as a lion, a powerful foe to contend with indeed, and as swift as an eagle, gathering together his forces to prepare them for the battle. And as it would swell our address too full to mention all the tribes in Philip's train of warriors, suffice it to say that from six to seven were with him at different times. When he begins the war, he goes forward and musters about 500 of his men and arms them complete, and about 900 of the other, making in all about fourteen hundred warriors when he commenced. It must be recollected that this war was legally declared by Philip, so that the colonies had a fair warning. It was no savage war of surprise, as some suppose, but one sorely provoked by the Pilgrims themselves. But when Philip and his men fought as they were accustomed to do and according to their mode of war, it was more than what could be expected. But we hear no particular acts of cruelty committed by Philip during the siege. But we find more manly nobility in him than we do in all the head Pilgrims put together, as we shall see during this quarrel between them. Philip's young men were eager to do exploits and to lead captive their haughty lords. It does appear that every Indian heart had been lighted up at the council fires, at Philip's speech, and that the forest was literally alive with this injured race. And now town after town fell before them. The Pilgrims with their forces were marching ever in one direction, while Philip and his forces were marching in another, burning all before them, until Middleborough, Taunton, and Dartmouth were laid in ruins and forsaken by its inhabitants.

At the great fight at Pocasset,[20] Philip commanded in person, where he also was discovered with his host in a dismal swamp. He had retired here with his army to secure a safe retreat from the Pilgrims, who were in close pursuit of him, and their numbers were so powerful they thought the fate of Philip was sealed. They surrounded the swamp, in hopes to destroy him and his army. At the edge of the swamp Philip had secreted a few of his men to draw them into ambush, upon which the Pilgrims showed fight, Philip's men retreating and the whites pursuing them till they were surrounded by Philip and nearly all cut off. This was a sorry time to them; the Pilgrims, however, reinforced but ordered a retreat, supposing it impossible for Philip to escape; and knowing his forces to be great, it was conjectured by some to build a fort to starve him out, as he had lost but few men in the fight. The situation of Philip was rather peculiar, as there was but one outlet to the swamp and a river before him nearly seven miles to descend. The Pilgrims placed a guard around the swamp for 13 days, which gave Philip and his men time to prepare

20. The battle began July 18, 1675. It started when fifteen Englishmen were killed in ambush in woods so thick that there was fear the English would shoot one another.

canoes to make good his retreat, in which he did, to the Connecticut River, and in his retreat lost but fourteen men. We may look upon this move of Philip's to be equal, if not superior, to that of Washington crossing the Delaware. For while Washington was assisted by all the knowledge that art and science could give, together with all the instruments of defense and edged tools to prepare rafts and the like helps for safety across the river, Philip was naked as to any of these things, possessing only what nature, his mother, had bestowed upon him; and yet makes his escape with equal praise. But he would not even [have] lost a man had it not been for Indians who were hired to fight against Indians, with promise of their enjoying equal rights with their white brethren; but not one of those promises have as yet been fulfilled by the Pilgrims or their children, though they must acknowledge that without the aid of Indians and their guides they must inevitably been swept off. It was only, then, by deception that the Pilgrims gained the country, as their word has never been fulfilled in regard to Indian rights.

Philip having now taken possession of the back settlements of Massachusetts, one town after another was swept off. A garrison being established at Northfield by the Pilgrims, and while endeavoring to reinforce it with thirty-six armed, twenty out of their number was killed and one taken prisoner. At the same time Philip so managed it as to cut off their retreat and take their ammunition from them.

About the month of August, they took a young lad about fourteen years of age, whom they intended to make merry with the next day; but the Pilgrims said God touched the Indians' heart, and they let him go. About the same time, the whites took an old man of Philip's, whom they found alone; and because he would not turn traitor and inform them where Philip was, they pronounced him worthy of death and by them was executed, cutting off first his arms and then his head. We wonder why God did not touch the Pilgrims' heart and save them from cruelty, as well as the Indians.

We would now notice an act in King Philip that outweighs all the princes and emperors in the world. That is, when his men began to be in want of money, having a coat neatly wrought with mampampeag (i.e., Indian money), he cut it to pieces and distributed it among all his chiefs and warriors, it being better than the old continental money of the Revolution in Washington's day, as not one Indian soldier found fault with it, as we could ever learn; so that it cheered their hearts still to persevere to maintain their rights and expel their enemies.

On the 18th of September, the Pilgrims made a tour from Hadley to Deerfield, with about eighty men, to bring their valuable articles of clothing and provisions. Having loaded their teams and returning, Philip and his men attacked them, and nearly slew them all. The attack was made near Sugarloaf

Hill.[21] It was said that in this fight the Pilgrims lost their best men of Essex and all their goods—upon which there were many made widows and orphans in one day. Philip now having done what he could upon the western frontiers of Massachusetts and believing his presence was wanted among his allies, the Narragansetts, to keep them from being duped by the Pilgrims, he is next known to be in their country.

The Pilgrims determined to break down Philip's power, if possible, with the Narragansetts: Thus they raised an army of 1,500 strong, to go against them and destroy them if possible. In this, Massachusetts, Plymouth, and Connecticut all join in severally, to crush Philip. Accordingly, in December, in 1675, the Pilgrims set forward to destroy them. Preceding their march, Philip had made all arrangements for the winter and had fortified himself beyond what was common for his countrymen to do, upon a small island near South Kingston, R.I. Here he intended to pass the winter with his warriors and their wives and children. About 500 Indian houses was erected of a superior kind, in which was deposited all their stores, tubs of corn, and other things, piled up to a great height, which rendered it bulletproof. It was supposed that 3,000 persons had taken up their residence in it. (I would remark that Indians took better care of themselves in those days than they have been able to since.) Accordingly, on the 19th day of December, after the Pilgrims had been out in the extreme cold for nearly one month, lodging in tents, and their provision being short, and the air full of snow, they had no other alternative than to attack Philip in the fort. Treachery, however, hastened his ruin; one of his men, by hope of reward from the deceptive Pilgrims, betrayed his country into their hands. The traitor's name was Peter. No white man was acquainted with the way, and it would have been almost impossible for them to have found it, much less to have captured it. There was but one point where it could have been entered or assailed with any success, and this was fortified much like a blockhouse, directly in front of the entrance, and also flankers to cover a crossfire—besides high palisades, an immense hedge of fallen trees of nearly a rod in thickness. Thus surrounded by trees and water, there was but one place that the Pilgrims could pass. Nevertheless, they made the attempt. Philip now had directed his men to fire, and every platoon of the Indians swept every white man from the path one after another, until six captains, with a great many of the men, had fallen. In the meantime, one Captain Moseley with some of his men had somehow or other gotten into the fort in another way and surprised them, by which the Pilgrims were enabled to capture the fort, at the same time setting fire to it and hewing down men, women, and children indiscriminately. Philip, however, was enabled to escape

21. Opposite present-day Sunderland, Massachusetts.

with many of his warriors. It is said at this battle eighty whites were killed and one hundred and fifty wounded, many of whom died of their wounds afterward, not being able to dress them till they had marched 18 miles, also leaving many of their dead in the fort. It is said that 700 of the Narragansetts perished, the greater part of them being women and children.

It appears that God did not prosper them much, after all. It is believed that the sufferings of the Pilgrims were without a parallel in history; and it is supposed that the horrors and burning elements of Moscow will bear but a faint resemblance of that scene. The thousands and ten thousands assembled there with their well-disciplined forces bear but little comparison to that of modern Europe, when the inhabitants, science, manners, and customs are taken into consideration. We might as well admit the above fact and say the like was never known among any heathen nation in the world; for none but those worse than heathens would have suffered so much, for the sake of being revenged upon those of their enemies. Philip had repaired to his quarters to take care of his people and not to have them exposed. We should not have wondered quite so much if Philip had gone forward and acted thus. But when a people calling themselves Christians conduct in this manner, we think they are censurable, and no pity at all ought to be had for them.

It appears that one of the whites had married one of Philip's countrymen; and they, the Pilgrims, said he was a traitor, and therefore they said he must die. So they quartered him; and as history informs us, they said, he being a heathen, but a few tears were shed at his funeral. Here, then, because a man would not turn and fight against his own wife and family, or leave them, he was condemned as a heathen. We presume that no honest men will commend those ancient fathers for such absurd conduct. Soon after this, Philip and his men left that part of the country and retired farther back, near the Mohawks, where, in July 1676, some of his men were slain by the Mohawks. Notwithstanding this, he strove to get them to join him; and here it is said that Philip did not do that which was right, that he killed some of the Mohawks and laid it to the whites in order that he might get them to join him. If so, we cannot consistently believe he did right. But he was so exasperated that nothing but revenge would satisfy him. All this act was no worse than our political men do in our days, of their strife to wrong each other, who profess to be enlightened; and all for the sake of carrying their points. Heathenlike, either by the sword, calumny, or deception of every kind; and the late duels among the [so-] called high men of honor is sufficient to warrant my statements. But while we pursue our history in regard to Philip, we find that he made many successful attempts against the Pilgrims, in surprising and driving them from their posts, during the year 1676, in February and through till August, in which time many of the Christian Indians joined him. It is thought by many that all would have joined him, if they had been left to their choice, as it appears they did not like their white brethren very well. It appears that Philip treated his prisoners with a great deal more Christian-like spirit than the Pilgrims did; even Mrs. Rowlandson,[22] although speaking with bitterness sometimes of the Indians, yet in her journal she speaks not a word against him. Philip even hires her to work for him, and pays her for her work, and then invites her to dine with him and to smoke with him. And we have many testimonies that he was kind to his prisoners; and when the English wanted to redeem Philip's prisoners, they had the privilege.

Now, did Governor Winthrop or any of those ancient divines use any of his men so? No. Was it known that they received any of their female captives into their houses and fed them? No, it cannot be found upon history. Were not the females completely safe, and none of them were violated, as they acknowledge themselves? But was it so when the Indian women fell into the hands of the Pilgrims? No. Did the Indians get a chance to redeem their prisoners? No. But when they were taken they were either compelled to turn traitors and join their enemies or be butchered upon the spot. And this is the dishonest method that the famous Captain Church used in doing his great exploits; and in no other way could he ever gained one battle.[23] So, after all, Church only owes his exploits to the honesty of the Indians, who told the truth, and to his own deceptive heart in duping them. Here it is to be understood that the whites have always imposed upon the credulity of the Indians. It is with shame, I acknowledge, that I have to notice so much corruption of a people calling themselves Christians. If they were like my people, professing no purity at all, then their crimes would not appear to have such magnitude. But while they appear to be by profession more virtuous, their crimes still blacken. It makes them truly to appear to be like mountains filled with smoke, and thick darkness covering them all around.

But we have another dark and corrupt deed for the sons of Pilgrims to look at, and that is the fight and capture of Philip's son and wife and many of

22. Mary Rowlandson was captured, along with three of her children, by a group of Philip's allies in an attack that destroyed her home village of Lancaster, Massachusetts. She was ransomed after six months of living with Indian war parties. Her *Narrative* of her captivity, published in 1682, became almost instantly popular and inaugurated one of the most important genres in American literature. Apess has read the *Narrative* carefully because, despite speaking "with bitterness sometimes of the Indians," she does present a human and even fond portrait of Philip, one from which we can get a glimpse of the very considerable man to whom Apess pays tribute.

23. Benjamin Church was the most successful of the leaders of the forces of the United Colonies against Philip. His sympathy with the Indians, his close knowledge of them, and his careful wooing of groups who were either unfriendly to Philip or otherwise uncertain about the war enabled him, as Apess rightly argues, to succeed where most of the other English commanders failed—in part because of their disdain for the Indians and a refusal to consider their ways.

his warriors, in which Philip lost about 130 men killed and wounded; this was in August 1676. But the most horrid act was in taking Philip's son, about ten years of age, and selling him to be a slave away from his father and mother. While I am writing, I can hardly restrain my feelings, to think a people calling themselves Christians should conduct so scandalous, so outrageous, making themselves appear so despicable in the eyes of the Indians; and even now, in this audience, I doubt but there is men honorable enough to despise the conduct of those pretended Christians. And surely none but such as believe they did right will ever go and undertake to celebrate that day of their landing, the 22nd of December. Only look at it; then stop and pause: My fathers came here for liberty themselves, and then they must go and chain that mind, that image they professed to serve, not content to rob and cheat the poor ignorant Indians but must take one of the king's sons and make a slave of him. Gentlemen and ladies, I blush at these tales, if you do not, especially when they professed to be a free and humane people. Yes, they did; they took a part of my tribe and sold them to the Spaniards in Bermuda, and many others;[24] and then on the Sabbath day, these people would gather themselves together and say that God is no respecter of persons; while the divines would pour forth, "He says that he loves God and hates his brother is a liar, and the truth is not in him"—and at the same time they hating and selling their fellow men in bondage. And there is no manner of doubt but that all my countrymen would have been enslaved if they had tamely submitted. But no sooner would they butcher every white man that come in their way, and even put an end to their own wives and children, and that was all that prevented them from being slaves; yes, *all*. It was not the good will of those holy Pilgrims that prevented. No. But I would speak, and I could wish it might be like the voice of thunder, that it might be heard afar off, even to the ends of the earth. He that will advocate slavery is worse than a beast, is a being devoid of shame, and has gathered around him the most corrupt and debasing principles in the world; and I care not whether he be a minister or member of any church in the world—no, not excepting the head men of the nation. And he that will not set his face against its corrupt principles is a coward and not worthy of being numbered among men and Christians—and conduct, too, that libels the laws of the country, and the word of God, that men profess to believe in.

After Philip had his wife and son taken, sorrow filled his heart, but notwithstanding, as determined as ever to be revenged, though [he] was

24. At the end of the Pequot War of 1637 the English sold a number of Pequots, men, women, and children, into slavery in Bermuda as part of their determination to wipe out the culture so they would never again be at risk of being challenged by it. The Pequots on Bermuda, though long out of touch with their New England brethren, have maintained a somewhat distinctive cultural identity to the present.

pursued by the duped Indians and Church into a swamp, one of the men proposing to Philip that he had better make peace with the enemy, upon which he slew him upon the spot. And the Pilgrims, being also repulsed by Philip, were forced to retreat with the loss of one man in particular, whose name was Thomas Lucas, of Plymouth. We rather suspect that he was some related to Lucas and Hedge, who made their famous speeches against the poor Marshpees, in 1834, in the Legislature, in Boston, against freeing them from slavery that their fathers, the Pilgrims, had made of them for years.

Philip's forces had now become very small, so many having been duped away by the whites and killed that it was now easy surrounding him. Therefore, upon the 12th of August, Captain Church surrounded the swamp where Philip and his men had encamped, early in the morning, before they had risen, doubtless led on by an Indian who was either compelled or hired to turn traitor. Church had now placed his guard so that it was impossible for Philip to escape without being shot. It is doubtful, however, whether they would have taken him if he had not been surprised. Suffice it to say, however, this was the case. A sorrowful morning to the poor Indians, to lose such a valuable man. When coming out of the swamp, he was fired upon by an Indian and killed dead upon the spot.

I rejoice that it was even so, that the Pilgrims did not have the pleasure of tormenting him. The white man's gun, missing fire, lost the honor of killing the truly great man, Philip. The place where Philip fell was very muddy. Upon this news, the Pilgrims gave three cheers; then Church ordering his body to be pulled out of the mud, while one of those tenderhearted Christians exclaims, "What a dirty creature he looks like." And we have also Church's speech upon that subject, as follows: "For as much as he has caused many a Pilgrim to lie above ground unburied, to rot, not one of his bones shall be buried." With him fell five of his best and most trusty men, one the son of a chief, who fired the first gun in the war.

Captain Church now orders him to be cut up. Accordingly, he was quartered and hung up upon four trees, his head and one hand given to the Indian who shot him, to carry about to show, at which sight it so overjoyed the Pilgrims that they would give him money for it, and in this way obtained a considerable sum. After which his head was sent to Plymouth and exposed upon a gibbet for twenty years; and his hand to Boston, where it was exhibited in savage triumph; and his mangled body denied a resting place in the tomb, and thus adds the poet,

> Cold with the beast he slew, he sleeps,
> O'er him no filial spirit weeps.

I think that, as a matter of honor, that I can rejoice that no such evil conduct is

"King Philip Dying for His Country" [frontispiece for the 1836 edition of *Eulogy on King Philip*]. This visual depiction is at odds with Apess's own description of how Metacomet died. He went to some length to imply that no whites unaided would ever have captured Metacomet and that they were "doubtless led on by an Indian who was either compelled or hired to turn traitor." Equally important in Apess's reading is that Metacomet be killed not by a white man but by an Indian: "When coming out of the swamp, he was fired upon by an Indian, and killed dead upon the spot." The engraving might represent what Apess emphasized about the whites' role in the mutilation of the great man's corpse: "he was quartered and hung up upon four trees; his head and one hand given to the Indian who shot him, to carry about to show. . . . After which his head was sent to Plymouth, and exposed upon a gibbet for twenty years."

Benjamin Church, the most successful of the colonial officers in the prosecution of the war and the commander of the troops that surrounded Metacomet (one of whose Indian allies shot the fatal bullet), kept a diary, which was later published by his son. Apess's account follows it closely. Courtesy, American Antiquarian Society.

recorded of the Indians, that they never hung up any of the white warriors who were head men. And we add the famous speech of Dr. Increase Mather; he says, during the bloody contest the pious fathers wrestled hard and long with their God, in prayer, that he would prosper their arms and deliver their enemies into their hands. And when upon stated days of prayer the Indians got the advantage, it was considered as a rebuke of divine providence (we suppose the Indian prayed best then), which stimulated them to more ardor.

And on the contrary, when they prevailed they considered it as an immediate interposition in their favor. The Doctor closes thus: "Nor could they, the Pilgrims, cease crying to the Lord against Philip, until they had prayed the bullet through his heart." And in speaking of the slaughter of Philip's people at Narragansett, he says, "We have heard of two and twenty Indian captains slain, all of them, and brought down to hell in one day." Again, in speaking of a chief who had sneered at the Pilgrims' religion, and who had withal added a most hideous blasphemy, "Immediately upon which a bullet took him in the head, and dashed out his brains, sending his cursed soul in a moment among the devils and blasphemers in hell forever." It is true that this language is sickening and is as true as the sun is in the heavens that such language was made use of, and it was a common thing for all the Pilgrims to curse the Indians, according to the order of their priests. It is also wonderful how they prayed, that they should pray the bullet through the Indians' heart and their souls down into hell. If I had any faith in such prayers, I should begin to think that soon we should all be gone. However, if this is the way they pray, that is, bullets through people's hearts, I hope they will not pray for me; I should rather be excused. But to say the least, there is no excuse for their ignorance how to treat their enemies and pray for them. If the Doctor and his people had only turned to the 23rd of Luke, and the 34th verse,[25] and heard the words of their Master, whom they pretended to follow, they would see that their course did utterly condemn them; or the 7th of Acts, and the 60th verse,[26] and heard the language of the pious Stephen, we think it vastly different from the Pilgrims; he prayed: "Lord, lay not this sin to their charge." No curses were heard from these pious martyrs.

I do not hesitate to say that through the prayers, preaching, and examples of those pretended pious has been the foundation of all the slavery and degradation in the American colonies toward colored people. Experience has taught me that this has been a most sorry and wretched doctrine to us poor ignorant Indians. I will mention two or three things to amuse you a little; that is, as I was passing through Connecticut, about 15 years ago, where they are so pious that they kill the cats for killing rats, and whip the beer barrels for working upon the Sabbath, that in a severe cold night, when the face of the earth was one glare of ice, dark and stormy, I called at a man's house to know if I could not stay with him, it being about nine miles to the house where I then lived, and knowing him to be a rich man, and withal very pious, knowing if he had a mind he could do it comfortably, and withal we were both members of

---

25. "Then Jesus said, 'Father, forgive them; for they know not what they do.'"
26. "Then he fell to his knees and cried out in a loud voice, 'Lord, do not hold this sin against them'; and when he said this, he fell asleep."

one church. My reception, however, was almost as cold as the weather, only he did not turn me out-of-doors; if he had, I know not but I should have frozen to death. My situation was a little better than being out, for he allowed a little wood but no bed, because I was an Indian. Another Christian asked me to dine with him and put my dinner behind the door; I thought this a queer compliment indeed.

About two years ago, I called at an inn in Lexington; and a gentleman present, not spying me to be an Indian, began to say they ought to be exterminated. I took it up in our defense, though not boisterous but coolly; and when we came to retire, finding that I was an Indian, he was unwilling to sleep opposite my room for fear of being murdered before morning. We presume his conscience pled guilty. These things I mention to show that the doctrines of the Pilgrims has grown up with the people.

But not to forget Philip and his lady, and his prophecy: It is (that is, 1671), when Philip went to Boston, his clothing was worth nearly one hundred dollars. It is said by some of the writers in those days that their money being so curiously wrought, that neither Jew nor devil could counterfeit it—a high encomium upon Indian arts; and with it they used to adorn their sagamores in a curious manner. It was said that Philip's wife was neatly attired in the Indian style; some of the white females used to call her a proud woman because she would not bow down to them and was so particular in adorning herself. Perhaps, while these ladies were so careful to review the queen, they had forgot that she was truly one of the greatest women there was among them, although not quite so white. But while we censure others for their faults in spending so much time to view their fair and handsome features, whether colored or white, we would remind all the fair sex it is what they all love, that is, jewels and feathers. It was what the Indian women used to love, and still love—and customs, we presume, that the whites brought from their original savage fathers, 1,000 years ago. Every white that knows their own history knows there was not a whit of difference between them and the Indians of their days.

But who was Philip, that made all this display in the world, that put an enlightened nation to flight and won so many battles? It was a son of nature, with nature's talents alone. And who did he have to contend with? With all the combined arts of cultivated talents of the Old and New World. It was like putting one talent against a thousand. And yet Philip, with that, accomplished more than all of them. Yea, he outdid the well-disciplined forces of Greece, under the command of Philip, the Grecian emperor; for he never was enabled to lay such plans of allying the tribes of the earth together, as Philip of Mount Hope did. And even Napoleon patterned after him, in collecting his forces and surprising the enemy. Washington, too, pursued many of his plans in attacking the enemy and thereby enabled him to defeat his antagonists and conquer them. What, then, shall we say? Shall we not do right to say that Philip, with his one talent, outstrips them all with their ten thousand? No warrior, of any age, was ever known to pursue such plans as Philip did. And it is well known that Church and nobody else could have conquered, if his people had not used treachery, which was owing to their ignorance; and after all, it is a fact that it was not the Pilgrims that conquered him; it was Indians. And as to his benevolence, it was very great; no one in history can accuse Philip of being cruel to his conquered foes; that he used them with more hospitality than they, the Pilgrims, did cannot be denied; and that he had knowledge and forethought cannot be denied. As Mr. Gookin,[27] in speaking of Philip, says, that he was a man of good understanding and knowledge in the best things. Mr. Gookin, it appears, was a benevolent man and a friend to Indians.

How deep, then, was the thought of Philip, when he could look from Maine to Georgia, and from the ocean to the lakes, and view with one look all his brethren withering before the more enlightened to come; and how true his prophecy, that the white people would not only cut down their groves but would enslave them. Had the inspiration of Isaiah been there, he could not have been more correct. Our groves and hunting grounds are gone, our dead are dug up, our council fires are put out, and a foundation was laid in the first Legislature to enslave our people, by taking from them all rights, which has been strictly adhered to ever since. Look at the disgraceful laws, disfranchising us as citizens. Look at the treaties made by Congress, all broken. Look at the deep-rooted plans laid, when a territory becomes a state, that after so many years the laws shall be extended over the Indians that live within their boundaries. Yea, every charter that has been given was given with the view of driving the Indians out of the states, or dooming them to become chained under desperate laws, that would make them drag out a miserable life as one chained to the galley; and this is the course that has been pursued for nearly two hundred years. A fire, a canker, created by the Pilgrims from across the Atlantic, to burn and destroy my poor unfortunate brethren, and it cannot be denied. What, then, shall we do? Shall we cease crying and say it is all wrong, or shall we bury the hatchet and those unjust laws and Plymouth Rock together and become friends? And will the sons of the Pilgrims aid in putting out the fire and destroying the canker that will ruin all that their fathers left behind them to destroy? (By this we see how true Philip spoke.) If so, we hope

27. Daniel Gookin was an early attendant among the Indians and of their history. His *Historical Collections of the Indians in New England* was published in 1792.

we shall not hear it said from ministers and church members that we are so good no other people can live with us, as you know it is a common thing for them to say Indians cannot live among Christian people; no, even the president of the United States tells the Indians they cannot live among civilized people, and we want your lands and must have them and will have them. As if he had said to them, "We want your land for our use to speculate upon; it aids us in paying off our national debt and supporting us in Congress to drive you off.

"You see, my red children, that our fathers carried on this scheme of getting your lands for our use, and we have now become rich and powerful; and we have a right to do with you just as we please; we claim to be your fathers. And we think we shall do you a great favor, my dear sons and daughters, to drive you out, to get you away out of the reach of our civilized people, who are cheating you, for we have no law to reach them, we cannot protect you although you be our children. So it is no use, you need not cry, you must go, even if the lions devour you, for we promised the land you have to somebody else long ago, perhaps twenty or thirty years; and we did it without your consent, it is true. But this has been the way our fathers first brought us up, and it is hard to depart from it; therefore, you shall have no protection from us." Now, while we sum up this subject, does it not appear that the cause of all wars from beginning to end was and is for the want of good usage? That the whites have always been the aggressors, and the wars, cruelties, and bloodshed is a job of their own seeking, and not the Indians? Did you ever know of Indians hurting those who was kind to them? No. We have a thousand witnesses to the contrary. Yea, every male and female declare it to be the fact. We often hear of the wars breaking out upon the frontiers, and it is because the same spirit reigns there that reigned here in New England; and wherever there are any Indians, that spirit still reigns; and at present, there is no law to stop it. What, then, is to be done? Let every friend of the Indians now seize the mantle of Liberty and throw it over those burning elements that has spread with such fearful rapidity, and at once extinguish them forever. It is true that now and then a feeble voice has been raised in our favor. Yes, we might speak of distinguished men, but they fall so far short in the minority that it is heard but at a small distance. We want trumpets that sound like thunder, and men to act as though they were going at war with those corrupt and degrading principles that robs one of all rights, merely because he is ignorant and of a little different color. Let us have principles that will give everyone his due; and then shall wars cease, and the weary find rest. Give the Indian his rights, and you may be assured war will cease.

But by this time you have been enabled to see that Philip's prophecy has come to pass; therefore, as a man of natural abilities, I shall pronounce him the greatest man that was ever in America; and so it will stand, until he is proved to the contrary, to the everlasting disgrace of the Pilgrims' fathers.

We will now give you his language in the Lord's Prayer.

Noo-chun kes-uk-qut-tiam-at-am unch koo-we-su-onk, kuk-ket-as-soo-tam-oonk pey-au-moo-utch, keet-te-nan-tam-oo-onk ne nai; ne-ya-ne ke-suk-qutkah oh-ke-it; aos-sa-ma-i-in-ne-an ko-ko-ke-stik-o-da-e nut-as-e-suk-ok-ke fu-tuk-qun-neg; kah ah-quo-an-tam-a-i-in-ne-an num-match-e-se-ong-an-on-ash, ne-match-ene-na-mun wonk neet-ah-quo-antam-au-o-un-non-og nish-noh pasuk noo-na-mortuk-quoh-who-nan, kah chaque sag-kom-pa-ginne-an en qutch-e-het-tu-ong-a-nit, qut poh-qud-wus-sin-ne-an watch match-i-tut.

Having now given historical facts, and an exposition in relation to ancient times, by which we have been enabled to discover the foundation which destroyed our common fathers in their struggle together; it was indeed nothing more than the spirit of avarice and usurpation of power that has brought people in all ages to hate and devour each other. And I cannot, for one moment, look back upon what is past and call it religion. No, it has not the least appearance like it. Do not then wonder, my dear friends, at my bold and unpolished statements, though I do not believe that truth wants any polishing whatever. And I can assure you that I have no design to tell an untruth, but facts alone. Oft have I been surprised at the conduct of those who pretend to be Christians, to see how they were affected toward those who were of a different cast, professing one faith. Yes, the spirit of degradation has always been exercised toward us poor and untaught people. If we cannot read, we can see and feel; and we find no excuse in the Bible for Christians conducting toward us as they do.

It is said that in the Christian's guide, God is merciful, and they that are his followers are like him. How much mercy do you think has been shown toward Indians, their wives, and their children? Not much, we think. No. And ye fathers, I will appeal to you that are white. Have you any regard for your wives and children, for those delicate sons and daughters? Would you like to see them slain and lain in heaps, and their bodies devoured by the vultures and wild beasts of prey, and their bones bleaching in the sun and air, till they molder away or were covered by the falling leaves of the forest, and not resist? No. Your hearts would break with grief, and with all the religion and knowl-edge you have, it would not impede your force to take vengeance upon your foe that had so cruelly conducted thus, although God has forbid you in so doing. For he has said, "Vengeance is mine, and I will repay." What, then, my dear affectionate friends, can you think of those who have been so often betrayed, routed, and stripped of all they possess, of all their kindred in the flesh? Can or do you think we have no feeling? The speech of Logan,[28] the white man's friend, is no doubt fresh in your memory, that he intended to live and die the friend of the white man; that he always fed them and gave them the best his cabin afforded; and he appealed to them if they had not been well used, to which they never denied. After which they murdered all of his family in cool blood, which roused his passions to be revenged upon the whites. This circumstance is but one in a thousand.

Upon the banks of Ohio, a party of two hundred white warriors, in 1757 or about that time, came across a settlement of Christian Indians and falsely accused them of being warriors, to which they denied, but all to no purpose; they were determined to massacre them all. They, the Indians, then asked liberty to prepare for the fatal hour. The white savages then gave them one hour, as the historian said. They then prayed together; and in tears and cries, upon their knees, begged pardon of each other, of all they had done, after which they informed the white savages that they were now ready. One white man then begun with a mallet and knocked them down and continued his work until he had killed fifteen, with his own hand; then, saying it ached, he gave his commission to another. And thus they continued till they had massacred nearly ninety men, women, and children, all these innocent of any crime. What sad tales are these for us to look upon the massacre of our dear fathers, mothers, brothers, and sisters; and if we speak, we are then called savages for complaining. Our affections for each other are the same as yours; we think as much of ourselves as you do of yourselves. When our children are sick, we do all we can for them; they lie buried deep in our affections; if they die, we remember it long and mourn in after years. Children also cleave to their parents; they look to them for aid; they do the best they know how to do for each other; and when strangers come among us, we use them as well as we know how; we feel honest in whatever we do; we have no desire to offend anyone. But when we are so deceived, it spoils all our confidence in our

28. Logan's speech, made after having his home and family destroyed by the English in 1774, was often quoted in this period as follows: "I appeal to any white to say, if ever he entered Logan's cabin hungry, and he gave him not meat; if ever he came cold and naked, and he clothed him not. During the course of the last long bloody war, Logan remained idle in his cabin, an advocate for peace. Such was my love for the whites that my countrymen pointed as they passed and said, 'Logan is the friend of the white men.' I had even thought to have lived with you, but for the injuries of one man. Col. Cresap, the last spring, in cold blood, and unprovoked, murdered all the relations of Logan; not even sparing my women and children. There runs not a drop of my blood in the veins of any living creature. This called on me for revenge. I have sought it. I have killed many. I have fully glutted my vengeance. For my country, I rejoice at the beams of peace. But do not harbor a thought that mine is the joy of fear. Logan never felt fear. He will not turn on his heel to save his life. Who is there to mourn for Logan?—Not one!"

visitors. And although I can say that I have some dear, good friends among white people, yet I eye them with a jealous eye, for fear they will betray me. Having been deceived so much by them, how can I help it? Being brought up to look upon white people as being enemies and not friends, and by the whites treated as such, who can wonder? Yes, in vain have I looked for the Christian to take me by the hand and bid me welcome to his cabin, as my fathers did them, before we were born; and if they did, it was only to satisfy curiosity and not to look upon me as a man and a Christian. And so all of my people have been treated, whether Christians or not. I say, then, a different course must be pursued, and different laws must be enacted, and all men must operate under one general law. And while you ask yourselves, "What do they, the Indians, want?" you have only to look at the unjust laws made for them and say, "They want what I want," in order to make men of them, good and wholesome citizens. And this plan ought to be pursued by all missionaries or not pursued at all. That is not only to make Christians of us, but men, which plan as yet has never been pursued. And when it is, I will then throw my might upon the side of missions and do what I can to favor it. But this work must begin here first, in New England.

Having now closed, I would say that many thanks is due from me to you, though an unworthy speaker, for your kind attention; and I wish you to understand that we are thankful for every favor; and you and I have to rejoice that we have not to answer for our fathers' crimes; neither shall we do right to charge them one to another. We can only regret it, and flee from it; and from henceforth, let peace and righteousness be written upon our hearts and hands forever, is the wish of a poor Indian.

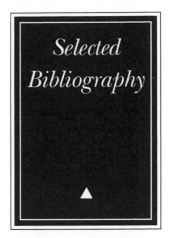

Selected Bibliography

Apess, William. *On Our Own Ground: The Complete Works of William Apess, A Pequot.* Edited and with an introduction by Barry O'Connell. Amherst: University of Massachusetts Press, 1992.

Calloway, Colin G., ed. *After King Philip's War: New Essays in New England Native American History.* Hanover: University Press of New England, 1997.

Cave, Alfred A. *The Pequot War.* Amherst: University of Massachusetts Press, 1996.

Clements, William M. *Native American Verbal Art: Texts and Contexts.* Tucson: University of Arizona Press, 1996.

Clifford, James. "Identity in Mashpee." In *The Predicament of Culture: Twentieth-Century Ethnography, Literature, and Art.* Cambridge: Harvard University Press, 1988.

Grumet, Robert S. *Historic Contact: Indian People and Colonists in Today's Northeastern United States in the Sixteenth through Eighteenth Centuries.* Norman: University of Oklahoma Press, 1995.

——, ed. *Northeastern Indian Lives, 1632–1816.* Amherst: University of Massachusetts Press, 1995.

Hauptman, Laurence M., and James D. Wherry, eds. *The Pequots in Southern New England: The Fall and Rise of an American Indian Nation.* Norman: University of Oklahoma Press, 1990.

Jaskowski, Helen, ed. *Early Native American Writing: New Critical Essays.* New York: Cambridge University Press, 1996.

Krupat, Arnold. *For Those Who Came After: A Study of Native American Autobiography.* Berkeley: University of California Press, 1985.

——. *The Voice in the Margin: Native American Literature and the Canon.* Berkeley: University of California Press, 1989.

Murray, David. *Forked Tongues: Speech, Writing and Representation in North American Indian Texts.* Bloomington: Indiana University Press, 1991.

O'Brien, Jean M. *Dispossession by Degrees: Indian Land and Identity in Natick, Massachusetts, 1650–1790.* New York: Cambridge University Press, 1997.

Pearce, Roy Harvey. *Savagism and Civilization: A Study of the Indian and the American Mind.* 1953. Revised ed., Berkeley: University of California Press, 1988.

Simmons, William S. *Spirit of the New England Tribes: Indian History and Folklore, 1620–1984.* Hanover: University Press of New England, 1986.

Walker, Cheryl. *Indian Nation: Naive American Literature and Nineteenth-Century Nationalism.* Durham, N.C.: Duke University Press, 1997.

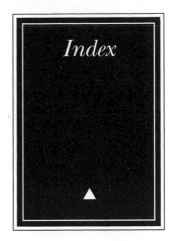

Index

Adam, 4, 10, 34

African Americans, x, xvi; in WA's writing, 37, 65, 95–100; intermarriage with Native Americans, 17; shared communities with Native Americans, 46, 51

Albany, N.Y., 26; WA preaching at, 49, 50–51; Methodist Episcopal Conference at, 51, 53–54

Alcohol: introduction of, by whites, 7, 53, 61; whites' trade to Native Americans, 33

Alcoholism, 25, 47; WA's, 25, 31–32, 35–37; WA's grandmother's, 5–6, 60–61; WA's parents, 60; among Native Americans, 7, 35; promoted by whites among Native Americans, 57

Alexander (Massasoit's son, Pokanoket), 111–12 and n.11, 118, 119

American Bible Society, 34 n

Apes, Candace (WA's mother, Pequot), xi and n, 4, 60

Apes, Erwin (WA's great-grandson), xix n

Apes, William (WA's father, Pequot), xi n, 4–5, 16, 23, 42–43, 60

Apes, William Elisha (WA's son, 1822?–1891, Pequot), xix n

Apess, Elizabeth (WA's second wife), xxi–xxii

Apess, Mary Wood (WA's first wife, 1788–?, Pequot), xvi and n, xxii, 46, 73–84; baptized, 82; birth and parentage, 73; bound out, 73–74; conversion experience, 74–83; despair, 78–79; as orphan, 74–75; spiritual temptations, 74–77; treatment of, 52–53

Apess, William (Pequot).
—biography: adulthood outlined, 70–73; alcoholism, 25, 31–32, 35–37; beatings and floggings, 6, 12, 13–14, 16, 17, 22, 60–61; with Canadian Indians, 31, 32–35, 71; childhood, 4–7, 59–62; children, 47; experiences of poverty, 5, 6, 60; grandparents, 5–7, 60–61 (maternal), 3–4, 6 (paternal); guardians, xi–xiii, 6–7, 9–15, 61–63 (Furmans), xiii, 14–16, 63–64 (Hillhouse), xiii–xiv, 16–23, 64–70 (W. Williamses); illnesses and injuries, 6, 7, 13–14, 22, 61; jobs, xv, 31–32, 35–36, 37, 41, 43, 46, 47, 48; journey from Canada, 35–37, 71; life after 1838, xxi–xxii; married, 46 and n.45; as orphan, 46, 47, 63, 64, 71, 72; problems in documenting biography, xv–xviii, xix, xxii; public career, 43–52, 72–73; runaway, xiii–xiv, 14, 16, 17, 22–25, 26–27, 63, 70; siblings, 5, 47 and n.46; spelling of name, xi n; uncle, 5–6, 61; in War of 1812, 26–31, 70–71; youth, 15–26, 63–70
—Mashpee and Mashpee Revolt, ix, xix–xxi
—and Methodists, xiii–xiv, 1; baptism (1818), xv, 42, 72; exhorter and preacher, xvi, xix–xx, 41, 43–46, 47–51, 72–73, 91; in Mashpee, xx–xxi; in his youth, xiii–xiv, 18–22, 65–70
—race and identity: WA and African Americans, 37, 65, 95–100; experiences of racism, 10, 12, 36, 60, 63, 64, 70, 72; forging an identity